WORDS TO LIVE BY

# CONFUCIUS SPEAKS

TSAI CHIH CHUNG

TRANSLATED BY BRIAN BRUYA

ANCHOR BOOKS
Doubleday
New York London Toronto Sydney Auckland

AN ANCHOR BOOK
PUBLISHED BY DOUBLEDAY
a division of Bantam Doubleday Dell Publishing Group, Inc.
1540 Broadway, New York, New York 10036

ANCHOR BOOKS, DOUBLEDAY, and the portrayal of an anchor are
trademarks of Doubleday, a division of Bantam Doubleday Dell
Publishing Group, Inc.

Library of Congress Cataloging-in-Publication Data
Ts'ai, Chih-chung, 1948–
Confucius speaks: words to live by/adapted and illustrated by
Tsai Chih Chung; translated by Brian Bruya.
p. cm.
1. Confucius—Comic books, strips, etc. I. Bruya, Brian, 1966– .
II. Title.
B128.C8T727 1996
181'.112—dc20      95-45157
CIP

ISBN 0-385-48034-2

# Contents

| | | | | |
|---|---|---|---|---|
| *Translator's Preface* | 7 | | Yan Hui's Intellect | 80 |
| *Introduction* | 9 | | You Can't Carve Rotten Wood | 81 |
| | | | The Meaning of "Cultured" | 82 |
| The Life of Confucius | 23 | | Contriving Appearances | 83 |
| The Analects | 67 | | Wishes | 84 |
| Pleasure and Humility | 68 | | A Town of Ten Families | 85 |
| Self-Critique | 69 | | Yan Hui's Learning | 86 |
| Like the North Star | 70 | | Yan Hui's Worthiness | 87 |
| Cultivating the Way | 71 | | The Wise and the Benevolent | 88 |
| True Understanding | 72 | | Transmitting Ideas | 89 |
| Proper Ceremony | 73 | | A Scholar's Ease | 90 |
| The Sacrificial Goat | 74 | | Dreaming of the Duke of Zhou | 91 |
| The Way of Self-Respect | 75 | | The Foundation of Good Conduct | 92 |
| What It Takes | 76 | | Universal Education | 93 |
| Seeing Yourself in Others | 77 | | Teaching Good Students | 94 |
| Traveling | 78 | | Simple Pleasures | 95 |
| Friends of Virtue | 79 | | Knowledge and Study | 96 |

| | | | |
|---|---|---|---|
| Learning from Others | 97 | A Good Horse | 120 |
| Fair Play | 98 | How to Treat One's Enemies | 121 |
| Dying Men Don't Lie | 99 | Understanding Confucius | 122 |
| Good Students Fear Forgetting | 100 | Stubborn | 123 |
| The Stream of Time | 101 | A Wasted Life | 124 |
| Age and Respect | 102 | Conditional Service | 125 |
| Facing Facts | 103 | Cultivating Benevolence | 126 |
| Fire in the Stable | 104 | Thinking Ahead | 127 |
| Spirits and Death | 105 | The Golden Rule | 128 |
| Overdoing It | 106 | Thinking vs. Studying | 129 |
| Chai Is Naïve | 107 | Yield to No One | 130 |
| Benevolence | 108 | The Three Temptations | 131 |
| Brothers | 109 | The Nine Considerations | 132 |
| The People's Trust | 110 | Praising Deeds | 133 |
| Assist in the Good | 111 | Nature vs. Nurture | 134 |
| Making Friends | 112 | The Six Defects | 135 |
| Rectifying Oneself | 113 | The Brazen Burglar | 136 |
| Patience and Prescience | 114 | Confucius and Ru Bei | 137 |
| Greed Is Shameful | 115 | Playing Games | 138 |
| The Complete Person | 116 | Maids and Valets | 139 |
| Saying and Doing | 117 | An Immature Forty | 140 |
| Extravagant in Deeds | 118 | Benevolence and Duty | 141 |
| Throwing Stones | 119 | Crazy Jieyu | 142 |

| | | | |
|---|---|---|---|
| The Two Recluses | 143 | Pu Shang | 155 |
| Being an Example | 146 | Tantai Mieming | 156 |
| The Disciples of Confucius | 147 | Zeng Shen | 157 |
| Yan Hui | 149 | You Ruo | 158 |
| Min Sun | 150 | Nangong Kuo | 159 |
| Ran Yong | 151 | Gongxi Chi | 160 |
| Zhong You | 152 | | |
| Zai Yu | 153 | *Guide to Pronunciation* | *161* |
| Duanmu Si | 154 | *Glossary* | *171* |

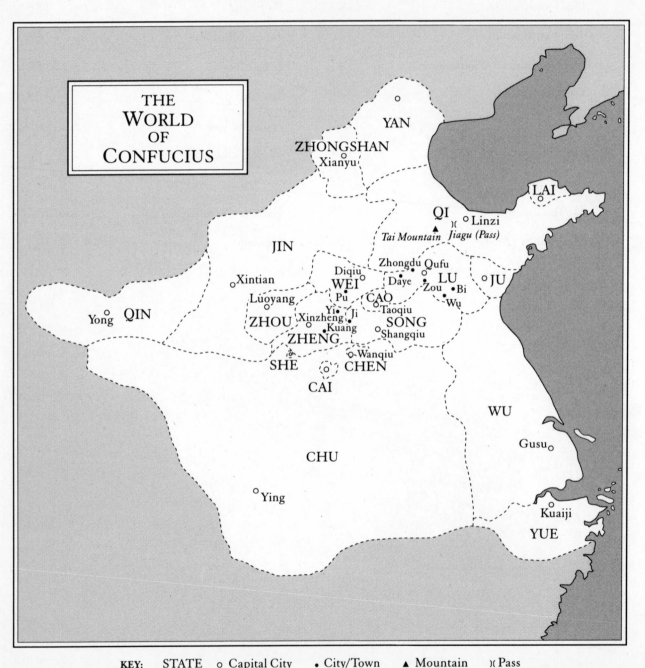

THE
WORLD
OF
CONFUCIUS

YAN

ZHONGSHAN
Xianyu

LAI

QI )( Linzi
Tai Mountain Jiagu (Pass)

JIN

Zhongdu Qufu
Diqiu
Xintian          WEI        Daye      LU
                                Zou  • Bi    JU
Luoyang    Pu       CAO           • Wu
Yong  QIN  ZHOU  Yi • Ji    Taoqiu
              Xinzheng        SONG
                 Kuang    Shangqiu
              ZHENG
                    Wanqiu
        SHE       CHEN

           CAI

                              WU

                                  Gusu

        CHU

           Ying

                          Kuaiji
                       YUE

KEY:    STATE    ○ Capital City    • City/Town    ▲ Mountain    )( Pass

# Translator's Preface

The novelty of an illustrated version of a Chinese classic deserves a brief explanation.

Tsai Chih Chung (C. C. Tsai) is the most accomplished and popular cartoonist in all of East Asia, with parts of this series of his books having even been incorporated into the public school curriculum in Japan. C. C. Tsai began his career at the age of sixteen by publishing the first of what would be approximately two hundred "action" comic books. Following that, he went into animation and garnered himself the Chinese equivalent of our Oscar while building up the largest animation company in Taiwan. In his spare time, he turned to the humor of comic strips and put out the first daily comic strip in Taiwan newspapers.

Then, one day on a flight to Japan, he began to sketch scenes from a book he was reading. The book had been written over two thousand years ago by one of the most influential thinkers in Chinese history, the famous Daoist (Taoist) named Zhuangzi (Chuang Tzu). From these sketches emerged a new genre in the book world—a serious (though light-hearted) comic book explicating a profound topic. C.C.'s aim was not to simplify, but to clarify. The ancient language of China is difficult for modern people to understand, so in addition to illustrating the subject matter, he also rendered the text into modern Chinese.

When *Zhuangzi Speaks* came out in Taiwan, it shot to the top of the bestseller list, and the head of a major publishing company immediately remarked that it had world potential. Tired of animation by now, C.C. sold off his company and devoted all of his efforts to the daily comic strips and his new series on ancient Chinese thought, both of which were bringing him unparalleled fame for a cartoonist. Soon, he held the four highest spots atop the bestseller list, until other authors demanded that comic books no longer be allowed on the list of "serious literature." There are now over twenty books in C.C.'s series and millions of copies in print, and, just as predicted, they are rapidly gaining popularity all over the world.

*Confucius Speaks* is an illustrated version of selected passages from the *Analects* of Confucius, one of the most influential books in Chinese history. This book, however, is not meant just as an illustration of how the Chinese mind works, but as a philosophical source book that still has much to offer the reader of modern times.

Beauty, love, goodness—these are a few of the ideals put forth over the centuries in the West, acclaimed, attacked, explained, turned around, analyzed, dissected, expostulated, and explained again. They are now so pregnant with meaning that to translate them into just one word in another language, especially a language where the same philosophical arguments that gave them their definitions never took place, is a difficult task. A parallel task is undertaken when translating traditional Chinese philosophical concepts into English.

Still, it must be attempted. The philosophical terms to look out for in this book are: propriety, benevolence, righteousness, virtue, conscientiousness, filial virtue, thoughtfulness, the Way, Heaven, gentleman, and worthy. Despite a translator's best efforts, there will always remain instances where the English word and the Chinese word will not entirely overlap in meaning, so for those who would like a clearer understanding of the subtleties of these terms, I refer you to Professor Ames' Introduction and the Glossary at the back of this book.

There are several places (p. 101, for instance) where C.C. draws what looks like a tiny, gleaming hat. This is actually a depiction of a Chinese ingot—a quantity of precious metal, symbolic here of treasure or wealth.

The panels at the margin of each page appeared in the Chinese version as supplementary material. We retain them not because the information is essential but primarily because they add a nice decorative touch to the book.

Many thanks, again, to Professor Lian Xinda for vetting the manuscript and offering numerous useful corrections. Thanks also to Professor Roger Ames for providing a lucid and enlightening Introduction.

—B.B.

# Introduction
# Confucius: His Life and Times

## The Historical Context

Confucius (551–479 B.C.) is arguably the most influential philosopher in human history. I say "is" rather than "was" because he is still very much alive.

Confucius is recognized as China's first teacher both chronologically and in importance; his ideas have been the rich soil in which the Chinese cultural tradition has grown and flourished. In fact, whatever we might mean by "Chineseness" today, some two and a half millennia after his death, is inseparable from the example of personal character that Confucius provided for posterity. And his influence did not end with China. All of the Sinitic cultures—especially Korea, Japan, and Vietnam—have evolved around ways of living and thinking derived from the wisdom of the Sage.

Confucius was born in the state of Lu in one of the most formative periods of Chinese culture. Two centuries before his birth, scores of small city-states owing their allegiance to the House of Zhou filled the Yellow River basin. This was the Zhou dynasty (ca. 1100–256 B.C.) out of which the empire of China was to emerge. By the time of Confucius' birth in the middle of the sixth century B.C., only fourteen independent states remained, with seven of the strongest elbowing each other militarily for hegemony over the central plains. It was a period of escalating internecine violence, driven by the knowledge that no state was exempt, and that all comers were competing in a zero-sum game—to fail to win was to perish. The accelerating ferocity of battle was like the increasing frequency and severity of labor pains, anticipating the eventual birth of the Chinese empire.

Not only was the landscape diverse politically. Intellectually, Confucius set a pattern for the "Hundred Schools" that emerged during these centuries in their competition for doctrinal supremacy. Confucius began the practice of independent philosophers traveling from state to state in an effort to persuade political leaders that their particular teachings were a practicable formula for social and political success. In the decades that followed the death of Confucius, intellectuals of every stripe—Confucians, Legalists, Mohists, Yin-yang Theorists, Militarists—would take to the road, attracted by court academies which sprang up to host them. Within these seats of learning, the viability of their various strategies for political and social unity would be hotly debated.

## Confucius as Teacher

A couple of centuries before Plato was to found his Academy to train statesmen for the political life of Athens, Confucius had established a school with the explicit purpose of educating the next generation for political leadership. Confucius is credited with having edited over his lifetime what were to become the Chinese classics, a collection of poetry, music, historical documents, and annals that chronicled the events at the Lu court, along with an extensive commentary on the *Book of Changes*. These classics provided a shared cultural vocabulary for his students, and were to become the standard curriculum for the Chinese literati in subsequent centuries. Although Confucius was deferred to

as a man of wisdom and culture by those around him, he described himself modestly as an avid student, and as a person who loved learning more than most.

As a teacher, Confucius expected this same degree of commitment to learning from his students. On the one hand, he was tolerant and inclusive. He made no distinction among the economic classes in selecting his students, and would take whatever they could afford in payment for his services. His favorite student, Yan Hui, was desperately poor, a fact that simply added to Confucius' admiration for him. On the other hand, Confucius set high standards, and if students did not approach their lessons with seriousness and enthusiasm, Confucius would not suffer them.

One stereotype of Chinese society and of Confucius in particular that is exploded by the passages selected for this book, *Confucius Speaks*, is the supposed reverence for age. Confucius did not promote an uncritical respect for age; instead, he respected accomplishment. In reflecting on the youth of his day, he said, "Young people should not be taken lightly; who's to say that someday they won't surpass our own generation?" And on confronting an old acquaintance who had lived a worthless life, Confucius rapped him with his cane, saying, "When you were young, you didn't understand humility or respect for elders.

As an adult, you had no accomplishments; and now you're old and refuse to die. What a disgrace!"

Over his lifetime, Confucius attracted a large group of young and able students, and provided them not only with book learning, but with a curriculum that encouraged personal articulation and refinement on several fronts. His "six arts" included propriety and ceremony, the making of music, archery, charioteering, writing, and mathematics, and, in sum, were directed at developing the moral character of his charges rather than any set of practical skills. In the Chinese tradition broadly, proficiency in the "arts" has been seen as the medium through which one reveals the quality of one's person.

Although Confucius enjoyed great popularity as a teacher and many of his students found their way into political office, his enduring frustration was that personally he achieved only marginal influence in the practical politics of the day. He was a *philosophe* rather than a theoretical philosopher; he wanted desperately to hold sway over intellectual and social trends, and to improve the quality of life that was dependent upon them. Although there were occasions on which important political figures sought his advice and services, throughout his years in the state of Lu, he held only minor offices at court. When finally Confucius was appointed as police commissioner of Lu, late in his career, his advice was not heeded, and he was not treated by the Lu court with appropriate courtesy. During his lifetime, Confucius had made several trips to neighboring states, and after being mistreated in the performance of court sacrifices at home, he determined to take his message on the road, and to try to influence the world outside. These were troubled times, and there were great adventure and much danger in offering counsel to the competing political centers of his day. In his early fifties, he traveled abroad as an itinerant counselor, and several times came under the threat of death. Having served briefly in Wei, he moved on to the states of Song and Cai, and took up office in the small state of Chen, only later to again return to service in the state of Wei. After his return to Wei, he was summoned back to Lu, where he lived out his last few years as a counselor of the lower rank and continued his compilation of the classics.

## Confucius as God

The early philosophical literature has a catalog of mostly apocryphal stories that purport to tell the events in the life of a remarkable man. Early on and certainly by the time of his death, Confucius had risen in reputation to become a model of erudition, attracting attention from all segments of society. Many of the stories that surround his life are intent on demonstrating how special a person Confucius was, and how different he was from the common run. Much of this material is an attempt to rationalize the few details that were known of his life. For example, there are several stories which describe the peculiar concave shape of his head, an attempt to explain his given name, *Giu*, meaning "mound" or "hill." Elaborate stories emerge out of offhand allusions in the historical records.

Another feature of this literature is Confucius' encounter with important men of his time. The assumption was that any sage worth his salt would certainly have attracted the attention of other sages. For example, in several historical texts and some of the Daoist literature, Confucius visits Laozi, sometimes receiving instruction from him, but more often being served discomfiture by him.

As time passes and the stock in Confucius rises, the historical records "recall" details about his official career that had supposedly been lost. Over time, his later disciples alter the wording of his biographical record in his favor, effectively promoting him from minor official to several of the highest positions in the land. He achieves the exalted rank first of acting Prime Minister of the state of Lu, and then Prime Minister. The later the record, the higher the position. What drives this exaggeration of Confucius' achievements is the conviction on the part of his later admirers that a person of his extraordinary talent could not possibly have lived among his community and been overlooked by the rulers of his day.

But the story does not end here. As the record moves into the Han dynasty, Confucius is celebrated as the "uncrowned king" of the state of Lu, and by the fourth century A.D., any prefecture wanting to define itself as a political entity is required by imperial decree to erect a temple to Confucius. Confucius is being treated *like* a god; gods in China are dead people. They are local cultural heroes who are remembered by history as having contributed meaning and value to the tradition. And of these revered ancestors, that god called Confucius has been remembered best.

## Confucius: His Influence

Confucius was certainly a flesh-and-blood historical figure, as real as Jesus or George Washington. But the received Confucius was and still is a "living corporate person" in the sense that generation after generation of descendants have written commentary on the legacy of Confucius in an effort to make his teachings appropriate for their own times and places. "Confucianism" is a lineage of scholars who have continued to elaborate upon the canonical texts passed on after the life of Confucius came to an end, extending the way of living that Confucius had begun. It is wave after wave of teachers who hold up the model of Confucius as an exemplar of what it means to become truly human.

Although the ascent of Confucius to exalted status began early in the tradition with the continuation of his work by his many disciples, it was not until Confucianism was established as the state ideology during the Han dynasty (206 B.C.–A.D. 200) that his school of thought became an unchallenged orthodoxy. By developing his insights around the most basic and enduring aspects of the human experience—family, friendship, education, community, and so on—Confucius has guaranteed their continuing relevance.

Two characteristics of Confucianism that began with Confucius himself, and made it so resilient in the Chinese tradition, are its porousness and adaptability. Confucius said of himself that he only transmitted traditional culture, he did not create it—his contribution was simply to take ownership of the tradition, and adapt the wisdom of the past to his own present his-torical moment. Confucius harks back to the Duke of Zhou, an idealized ruler who helped to establish the high culture of the Zhou dynasty in its first century, and on a bad day when things are not going well for Confucius, he laments, "It is a long time since I have dreamt of the Duke of Zhou."

Just as Confucius reinvented the culture of the Zhou and earlier dynasties for his own era, Han dynasty Confucianism draws into itself many of the ideas owned by competing schools in the earlier centuries, and in so doing, fortifies itself against their challenge. This pattern—absorbing competing ideas and adapting them to the specific conditions of the time—sustained Confucianism across the centuries as the official doctrine of the Chinese empire until the fall of the Qing dynasty in 1911. In fact, an argument can be made that just as the composite of Buddhism and Confucianism produced neo-Confucianism, the combination of Marxism and Confucianism in this century has created a kind of neo-neo-Confucianism.

As recently as the Cultural Revolution (1966–76), Mao Zedong's wife, Jiang Qing, and her cohorts mounted an anti-Confucius campaign that swept the country. Although the struggle was ostensibly between the Gang of Four–backed "Legalists" and the reactionary "Confucians," the real target was Premier Zhou

Enlai—a modern reincarnation of Confucius' cultural hero, the Duke of Zhou. The great irony of the anti-Confucius campaign was that during this period one could not buy a copy of the *Analects* for love or money—the entire country was put to work reading the teachings of Confucius in order to criticize them!

## The *Analects*: Sagely Leftovers

There are many sources for the teachings of Confucius that have been passed down to us today. Although *Confucius Speaks* draws from many of them in bringing the historical Confucius to life, for the actual teachings of Confucius, it relies primarily on the most authoritative among them, the *Analects*. "Analects" is a good translation of *"lunyu"*—literally "discourses"—because it comes from the Greek *analekta*, which has the root meaning of "leftovers after a feast." It is probably the case that the first fifteen books of these literary "leftovers" were assembled and edited by a congress of Confucius' disciples shortly after his death. It would seem the disciples concluded that a very special person had walked among them, and that his way—what he said and did—should be preserved for future generations. Much of this portion of the text is devoted to remembering Confucius—a personal narrative of what he had to say, to whom

he said it, and how he said it. The middle three chapters are like snapshots of his life-habits—Confucius never sat down without first straightening his mat; he never slept in the posture of a corpse; he never sang on a day that he attended a funeral; he drank freely, but never to the point of being confused of mind.

The last five books of the *Analects* appear to have been compiled sometime later, after the most prominent disciples of Confucius had launched their own teaching careers, and had taken it upon themselves to elaborate on the philosophy of their late Master. Confucius is less prominent in these chapters, yet he is referenced with more honorific terms, while the now mature disciples are themselves often quoted.

There were many versions of the *Analects*, with three important editions surviving into the Han dynasty: the Lu version from the state of Lu, the Qi version from the state of Qi, and the "Ancient" version reportedly recovered from within the walls of Confucius' old home. While the presently extant text is eclectic, having had access to all three versions, its editor had to make choices among them.

There is exciting news on this front. In 1971 a version of the *Analects* was recovered from a tomb dating from 55 B.C. in an archaeological dig just outside of Beijing. This *Analects* is a thousand years older than our received text, and we know from on-site reports that it is probably the Qi edition. It is substantially different from the text in circulation today, containing twenty-two books rather than twenty, having possibly additional and more elaborate passages within the existing twenty books, and having significant variations in the readings of extant passages. Although badly damaged by fire and only fragmentary (perhaps 70 percent of the original text), the potential that this find holds for revising our understanding of one of the most canonical texts in human history is at least comparable in importance to the discovery of the Dead Sea scrolls.

In addition to the *Analects*, the other two most important sources for the life and teachings of Confucius are the Zuo commentary on the *Spring and Autumn Annals*, and the *Mencius*. The Zuo commentary is a narrative history which purports to interpret the chronicle of the court history of the state of Lu up until the death of Confucius. *Mencius* is a text named after a disciple who elaborated the doctrines of Confucius some century and a half after his death, and it became one of the *Four Books* in the Song dynasty—from then on, the core of the Confucian classics.

One thing is clear about the *Analects* and these supplementary texts: they do not purport to lay out a formula that everyone should live by. Rather, they provide an account of one man: how he cultivated his humanity, and how he lived a satisfying life, much to the admiration of those around him.

## The Teachings of Confucius

The Way (*Dao*) of Confucius is nothing more or less than the way in which he, as a particular person, chose to live his life. The power and lasting value of his ideas lie in the fact that they are intuitively persuasive, and readily adaptable. Confucius begins from the insight that the life of every human being is played out within the context of his or her particular family, for better or for worse. For Confucius and generations of Chinese to come, it is one's family and the complex of relationships that constitute it, rather than the solitary individual, that are the basic unit of humanity. In fact, for Confucius, there is no individual—no "self" or "soul"—that remains once layer after layer of social relations is peeled away. One is one's roles and relationships. The goal of living, then, is to achieve harmony and enjoyment for oneself and others through acting appropriately in those roles and relationships that constitute one.

Given that we all live within the web of family relationships, it is entirely natural that we should project this institution out onto the community, the polity, and the cosmos as an organizing metaphor. The Confucian community is an extension of aunts and uncles, sisters and cousins; the teacher is "teacher-father," and one's senior classmates are "elder-brother students"; "the ruler is father and mother to the people, and is the son of 'Heaven.'" "Heaven" itself is a faceless amalgam of ancestors rather than some transcendent Creator deity. As Confucius says, "The gentleman works hard at the root, for where the root has taken firm hold, the way will grow." What then is the root? He continues: "Treating your family members properly—this is the root of becoming a person."

For Confucius, the way to live is not dictated for us by some power beyond; it is something we all must participate in constructing. On one occasion, Confucius said, "It is not the Way that broadens people, but people who broaden the Way." The Way is our passage through life, the road we take. Our forebears mapped out their way and built their roads, and, in so doing, have provided a bearing for succeeding generations. They have given us the culture and institutions that structure our lives and give them value and meaning. But each new generation must be road-builders too, and continue the efforts that have gone before.

Confucius saw living as an art rather than a science. There are no blueprints, no formulae, no replications. He once said, "The gentleman seeks harmony, not sameness." In a family, each member has his or her unique and particular role. Harmony is simply getting the most out of these differences. Similarly, Confucius saw harmony in community emerging out of the uninhibited contributions of its diverse people. Communal enjoyment is like Chinese cooking—getting the most out of your ingredients.

Confucius was extraordinarily fond of good music, because making music conduces to harmony, bringing different voices into productive relationships. Music is tolerant in allowing each voice and instrument to have its own place, its own integrity, while at the same time requiring that each ingredient find a complementary role in which it can add the most to the ensemble. And music is always unique in that each performance has a life of its own.

What Confucius calls "benevolence" (ren)—more literally, "becoming a person"—is the recognition that personal character is the consequence of cultivating one's relationships with others. There is nothing more defining of humanity for Confucius than the practical consideration of one human being for another. Important here, benevolence does not precede practical employment—it is not a principle or standard that has some existence beyond the day-to-day lives of the people who realize it in their relationships. Rather, benevolence is fostered in the deepening of relationships that occur as one takes on the responsibility and obligations of communal living, and comes fully to life. Benevolence is human flourishing. It is the achievement of the quality of relationships that, like the lines in calligraphy or landscape painting, collaborate to maximum aesthetic effect.

Wisdom for Confucius is relevant knowledge—not knowing "what" in some abstract and theoretical sense, but knowing "how" to map one's way through life and get the most happiness out of it. And happiness for oneself and for others is isomorphic; it is mutually entailing. In discussing knowledge, Confucius says that being fond of something is better than just knowing it, and finding enjoyment in it is better than just being fond of it. Benevolence Confucius associates with mountains—spiritual and enduring, a constant geographical marker from which we can all take our bearings. Wisdom is like water—pure, flowing, nurturing. And the gentleman is both benevolent and wise, both mountain and water.

A good way to think about "the Way" is the notion of passage. On one occasion, Confucius was standing on the bank of a river, and waxing philosophical, he said, "All things that pass are just like this! Night and day, it never stops." Life is at its very best a pleasant journey, where the inherited body of cultural institutions and the pattern of roles and relationships that locate us within the community—what Confucius calls "propriety" (*li*)—are a code of formal behaviors for stabilizing and disciplining our ever-changing circumstances. "Propriety" covers everything from table manners to the three years of mourning on the loss of one's parent, from the institution of parenthood to the appropriate posture for expressing commiseration. It is a social syntax that brings the particular members of the community into meaningful relationships. Propriety is a discourse, which, like language, enables people to communicate, and to locate themselves appropriately, one with the other.

What distinguishes "propriety" from rules and regulations is that these cultural norms must be personalized, and are open to refinement. Only I can be father to *my* sons; only I can be *this* son to *my* mother; only I can sacrifice to *my* ancestors. And if I act properly, performing my roles and cultivating my relationships so that they are rich and fruitful, other people in my community will see me as a model of appropriate conduct, and will defer. It is precisely this power of example that Confucius calls "virtue" (*de*). Virtue is the propensity of people to behave in a certain way when provided with an inspiring model.

The other side to what Confucius calls "propriety" is the cultivation of a sense of shame. Shame is community-based. It is an awareness of and a concern for how others perceive one's conduct. Persons with a sense of shame genuinely care about what other people think of them. Self-sufficient individuals, on the other hand, need not be concerned about the judgments of others. And such individuals can thus be capable of acting shamelessly, using any means at all to take what they want when they want it.

## The Disciples

Confucius was tolerant of difference. In fact, on six separate occasions in the *Analects*, he was asked what he means by "benevolence," an idea that is at the heart of his teachings. And six times Confucius gives different answers. For Confucius, instructing disciples in "benevolence" requires that the message be tailored to the conditions of the person asking the question. We have said that, for Confucius, persons are no more than the sum of their specific familial and communal roles and relationships, and that "benevolence" emerges out of the quality that they are able to achieve in cultivating them. It stands to reason, then, that to know Confucius, we do best to familiarize ourselves with his community of disciples. The Teacher can best be known by his students. Some of these disciples come to life in a careful reading of the *Analects*.

Confucius was reluctant to use the term "benevolent" to describe anyone, but he did use it for his favorite disciple, Yan Hui, also called Yan Yuan. Yan Hui lived on a bowl of rice and a ladle of water, and his eagerness to learn and his sincerity endeared him to the Master. But it was more, much more. Yan Hui was of incomparable character, and was so intelligent that Confucius said of him, "When he is told one thing he understands ten." Although Yan Hui was some thirty years younger than Confucius, it was only he among his many disciples that Confucius saw as his equal. It is no surprise, then, that Confucius was totally devastated at the death of Yan Hui at the young age of thirty-one.

Min Sun, known as Ziqian, was praised as an exemplary son, and was admired by Confucius for the economy and directness of his comments, and for his uncompromising scruples in refusing to serve persons of questionable morals.

Ran Yong, called Zhonggong, like Yan Hui, was three decades younger than Confucius. Although Zhonggong was of humble origins, Confucius thought so highly of him and his refinement that he said: "Zhonggong could be king"—high praise indeed!

Zhong You, also known as Zilu, was another of Confucius' best-known and favorite disciples. He was a person of courage and action who was sometimes upbraided by Confucius for being too bold and impetuous. When he asked Confucius if courage was indeed the highest virtue, Confucius tried to rein him in by replying that a person who has courage without a sense of appropriateness will be a troublemaker, and a lesser person will be a thief.

Confucius' feelings for Zilu were mixed. On the one hand, he was constantly critical of Zilu's rashness and immodesty, and impatient with his seeming indifference to book learning. On the other hand, Confucius appreciated Zilu's unswerving loyalty and directness—he never delayed in fulfilling his commitments.

But being nearer Confucius in age, Zilu with his military temper was not one to take criticism without giving it back. On several occasions, especially in the apocryphal literature, Zilu challenges Confucius' judgment in associating with political figures of questionable character and immodest reputation—the wife of Duke Ling of Wei, for example. Confucius is left defending himself—honest, I didn't do anything! At the end of the day, enormous affection for the irrepressible Zilu comes through the text.

Zai Yu, also called Ziwo, was devoted to Confucius, yet on numerous occasions, Confucius criticized him roundly for a lack of character.

Confucius, in a metaphorical reference to attempting to educate Ziwo, said you cannot carve rotten wood, nor can you whitewash a wall made from dry manure.

Duanmu Si, known as Zigong, excelled as a statesman and as a merchant, and was perhaps second only to Yan Hui in Confucius' affections. Confucius was respectful of Zigong's abilities, and in particular his intellect, but less impressed with Zigong's use of this intellect to amass personal wealth. Putting the many references to Zigong together, it is clear that Confucius was not entirely comfortable with his lack of commitment to the well-being of others, choosing to increase his own riches rather than take on the responsibilities of government office. Zigong was aloof, and not a generous man. And in his readiness to pass judgment on others, he acted superior. Coming from a wealthy, educated home, Zigong was well-spoken, and as such, Confucius' most persistent criticism of him was that his deeds could not keep pace with his words. Even so, much of the flattering profile of Confucius collected in the *Analects* is cast in the words of the eloquent Zigong.

Pu Shang, known as Zixia, was a man of letters, and is remembered by tradition as having had an important role in establishing the Confucian canon. He has a major place in the last five chapters, where he underscores the importance of learning. Confucius allows that he himself has gotten a great deal from his conversations with Zixia.

Although Zixia tries to compensate for his image as a pedant by insisting that virtuous conduct in one's personal relationships is what learning is all about, Confucius criticizes him at times for being petty and narrow in his aspirations.

Ziyu, whose formal name was Tantai Mieming, was a protégé of Ziyou, described below, and as such, invested a great deal of importance in protocol.

Zeng Can, known as Ziyu or Zengzi, is best remembered as a proponent of filial piety—devotion and service to one's parents. A natural extension of this affection for one's family is friendship, and Zengzi is portrayed as being able to distinguish between the sincerity of Yan Hui and the rashness of Zizhang.

If Zixia erred on the side of book learning, You Ruo, also known as Ziyou, went too far in the direction of Ziyu, emphasizing the formal side of the Confucian teachings, the rites and rituals, at the expense of warmth and good humor.

Nangong Gua, called Zirong, was a person whom Confucius praised as a gentleman and a man of virtue. He held office only when the Way prevailed in the land, and stayed out of harm's way when it did not. It is not surprising that Confucius gave his niece to him in marriage.

Gongxi Chi, also known as Zihua, has the image of a diplomat, careful and concise in his speech, and proper in his decorum.

These and many other disciples came from around the central states of China, gravitating to the state of Lu to study with Confucius. In spite of the sometimes severe opinions which Confucius expressed freely about them—and he admonishes almost every one of them—they were devoted to the Master, and responded to him with reverence. There is no greater proof of this enduring respect for Confucius than the fact that they had a hand in recording Confucius' criticisms of themselves, and then went on to found branch schools based on these same criticisms to perpetuate his teachings.

A revised draft of this essay will appear as an entry on Confucius in the *Encyclopedia of Chinese Philosophy*, edited by A. C. Cua for Garland Publishing, New York.

# Bibliography

Finagarette, Herbert A. *Confucius: The Secular as Sacred.* New York: Harper & Row, 1972. (A pioneering reevaluation of the philosophy of Confucius, and its relevance to contemporary philosophy.)

Hall, David L., and Roger T. Ames. *Thinking Through Confucius.* Albany, NY: State University of New York Press, 1987. (A reconstruction of the philosophical insights of Confucius, comparing the presuppositions of his way of thinking with presuppositions that underlie the Western traditions of philosophy.)

Lau, D. C. (trans.). *Confucius: The Analects (Lun-yü).* Hong Kong: Chinese University Press, 1992. (A revised bilingual translation of the *Analects*, complete with a philosophical introduction, appendices on the history of the text, events in the life of Confucius, and a characterization of his various disciples. The most authoritative English translation.)

Roger T. Ames
Director, Center for Chinese Studies,
University of Hawai'i

# The Life of Confucius

(FROM SIMA QIAN'S *THE HISTORIAN'S RECORDS,* 1ST CENTURY B.C.)

孔子生魯昌平鄉陬邑。其先宋人也，曰孔防叔。防叔生伯夏，伯夏生叔梁紇。紇與顏氏女野合而生孔子，禱於尼丘得孔子。魯襄公二十二年而孔子生。生而首上圩頂，故因名曰丘云。字仲尼，姓孔氏。

丘生而叔梁紇死，葬於防山。防山在魯東，由是孔子疑其父墓處，母諱之也。孔子為兒嬉戲，常陳俎豆，設禮容。孔子母死，乃殯五父之衢蓋其慎也。陬人輓父之母誨孔子父墓，然後往合葬於防焉。

孔子要絰，季氏饗士，孔子與往。陽虎絀曰：「季氏饗士，非敢饗子也。」孔子由是退。

23

# THE LIFE OF CONFUCIUS

CONFUCIUS WAS BORN IN THE TOWN OF ZOU, CHANGPING COUNTY, IN THE STATE OF LU IN THE 21st YEAR (551 B.C.) OF THE ZHOU KING LING, DURING CHINA'S SPRING & AUTUMN PERIOD OF THE ZHOU DYNASTY.

LU

CONFUCIUS' FATHER WAS KONG HE, WHO STOOD SIX FEET EIGHT INCHES TALL AND WAS UNSURPASSED IN STRENGTH. AFTER HIS FIRST WIFE HAD GIVEN BIRTH TO NINE DAUGHTERS, THE ELDER KONG HOPED DESPERATELY FOR A SON, AND ALTHOUGH THE NEXT CHILD BORN WAS MALE, HE TURNED OUT TO BE CRIPPLED.

SO AT SIXTY-FOUR YEARS OLD, KONG HE TOOK A YOUNG WOMAN OF THE SURNAME YAN AS HIS SECOND WIFE, AND SHE GAVE BIRTH TO KONG QIU, KNOWN TO LATER CHINESE AS KONGFUZI, MASTER KONG, LATINIZED AS CONFUCIUS.

WHEN CONFUCIUS WAS ONLY THREE YEARS OLD, HIS FATHER PASSED AWAY.

KONG HE R.I.P.

WHEN CONFUCIUS WAS A CHILD, HE PLAYED GAMES IN WHICH HE ARRANGED RITUAL VESSELS...

AND IMITATED THE CEREMONIAL GESTURES OF ADULTS.

24

AT FIFTEEN, HE SET HIS MIND ON LEARNING.

AT NINETEEN, HE MARRIED A WOMAN FROM SONG OF THE SURNAME BINGGUAN.

THE FOLLOWING YEAR, HE HAD A SON, WHOM HE NAMED KONG LI.

AT TWENTY YEARS OLD, CONFUCIUS WORKED AS MANAGER OF A GRANARY.

HE FIGURED THE ACCOUNTS WITH GREAT ACCURACY AND CLARITY.

HE ALSO HELD A MINOR MANAGERIAL POSITION AT A RANCH. AND UNDER HIS SUPERVISION, THE NUMBER OF ANIMALS STEADILY INCREASED.

LATER, HE ASSUMED THE OFFICE OF MINISTER OF PUBLIC WORKS.

孔子貧且賤。及長，嘗為季氏史，料量平；嘗為司職吏而畜蕃息。由是為司空。已而去魯，斥乎齊，逐乎宋、衛，困於陳蔡之間，於是反魯。孔子長九尺有六寸，人皆謂之「長人」而異之。魯復善待，由是反魯。

魯南宮敬叔言魯君曰：「請與孔子適周。」魯君與之一乘車，兩馬，一豎子俱，適周問禮，蓋見老子云。辭去，而老子送之曰：「吾聞富貴者送人以財，仁人者送人以言。吾不能富貴，竊仁人之號，送子以

25

言，曰：『聰明深察而近於死者，好議人者也。博辯廣大危其身者，發人之惡者也。為人子者毋以有己，為人臣者毋以有己。』」孔子自周反于魯，弟子稍益進焉。

是時也，晉平公淫，六卿擅權，東伐諸侯；楚靈王兵彊，陵轢中國；齊大而近於魯。魯小弱，附於楚則晉怒；附於晉則楚來伐；不備於齊，齊師侵魯。

魯昭公之二十年，而孔子蓋年三十矣。齊景公與晏嬰來適魯，景公問孔子曰：「昔秦穆公國小處辟，

IN THE TWENTIETH YEAR OF DUKE ZHAO OF LU, NANGONG JINGSHU RECOMMENDED THAT CONFUCIUS BE SENT TO ZHOU TO STUDY THE CEREMONIES.

WHILE STUDYING THE CEREMONIES IN ZHOU, CONFUCIUS PAID A VISIT TO LAOZI TO ASK HIM ABOUT THE CEREMONIES.

AFTER THEIR SESSION, LAOZI SENT HIM OFF WITH THESE WORDS:

THE WEALTHY SEND PEOPLE OFF WITH GIFTS, AND THE BENEVOLENT SEND PEOPLE OFF WITH WORDS. SINCE I AM NOT WEALTHY, I GIVE YOU THESE WORDS:

INTELLIGENT PEOPLE OFTEN ENCOUNTER TROUBLE BECAUSE THEY TEND TO CRITICIZE OTHERS. LEARNED PEOPLE OFTEN ENCOUNTER DANGER BECAUSE THEY TEND TO EXPOSE THE MISDEEDS OF OTHERS. CHILDREN SHOULD BE MINDFUL OF THEIR PARENTS, AND SUBORDINATES SHOULD BE MINDFUL OF THEIR SUPERIORS. DON'T ALWAYS THINK ONLY OF YOURSELF.

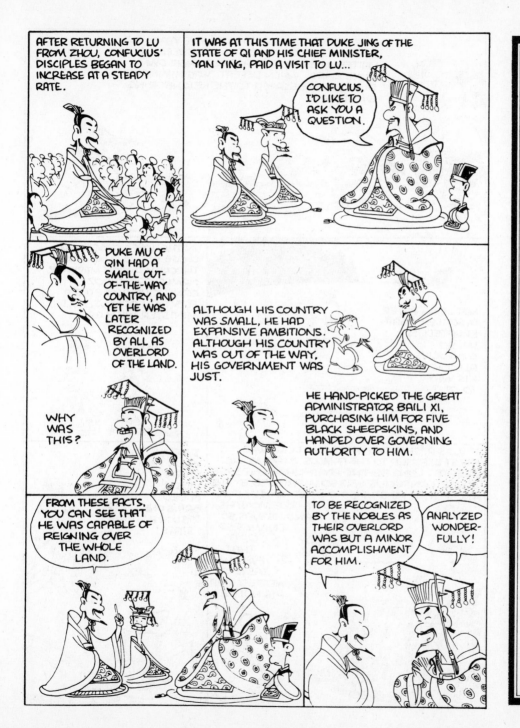

**Panel 1:** AFTER RETURNING TO LU FROM ZHOU, CONFUCIUS' DISCIPLES BEGAN TO INCREASE AT A STEADY RATE.

**Panel 2:** IT WAS AT THIS TIME THAT DUKE JING OF THE STATE OF QI AND HIS CHIEF MINISTER, YAN YING, PAID A VISIT TO LU...

CONFUCIUS, I'D LIKE TO ASK YOU A QUESTION.

**Panel 3:** DUKE MU OF QIN HAD A SMALL OUT-OF-THE-WAY COUNTRY, AND YET HE WAS LATER RECOGNIZED BY ALL AS OVERLORD OF THE LAND.

WHY WAS THIS?

**Panel 4:** ALTHOUGH HIS COUNTRY WAS SMALL, HE HAD EXPANSIVE AMBITIONS. ALTHOUGH HIS COUNTRY WAS OUT OF THE WAY, HIS GOVERNMENT WAS JUST.

HE HAND-PICKED THE GREAT ADMINISTRATOR BAILI XI, PURCHASING HIM FOR FIVE BLACK SHEEPSKINS, AND HANDED OVER GOVERNING AUTHORITY TO HIM.

**Panel 5:** FROM THESE FACTS, YOU CAN SEE THAT HE WAS CAPABLE OF REIGNING OVER THE WHOLE LAND.

**Panel 6:** TO BE RECOGNIZED BY THE NOBLES AS THEIR OVERLORD WAS BUT A MINOR ACCOMPLISHMENT FOR HIM.

ANALYZED WONDERFULLY!

其霸何也？」對曰：「秦，國雖小，其志大；處雖辟，行中正。身舉五羖，爵之大夫，起纍紲之中，與語三日，授之以政。以此取之，雖王可也，其霸小矣。」景公說。

孔子年三十五，而季平子與郈昭伯以鬥雞故得罪魯昭公，昭公率師擊平子，平子與孟氏、叔孫氏三家共攻昭公，昭公敗，奔於齊，齊處昭公乾侯。其後頃之，魯亂。孔子適齊，為高昭子家臣，欲以通乎景公。與齊太師語樂，聞韶音，學之，三月不知肉味，齊人稱之。

WHEN CONFUCIUS WAS THIRTY-FIVE YEARS OLD, THE THREE MOST POWERFUL LU NOBLEMEN UNITED IN AN ATTACK AGAINST THEIR OWN DUKE ZHAO. WHEN DEFEAT WAS IMMINENT, DUKE ZHAO ESCAPED TO THE NEIGHBORING QI STATE.

NOT LONG AFTER, DISORDER AGAIN ERUPTED IN LU, SO CONFUCIUS ALSO FOUND HIS WAY TO QI.

IN THE HOPES OF GETTING CLOSE TO QI'S DUKE JING THROUGH A HIGH MINISTER NAMED GAO ZHAOZI, CONFUCIUS ACCEPTED A POSITION AS HOUSEHOLD MINISTER WITH GAO.

IT WAS AT THIS TIME THAT CONFUCIUS WAS FIRST EXPOSED TO THE FAMOUS *SHAO* MUSIC CREATED LONG BEFORE BY THE ANCIENT SAGE SHUN. CONFUCIUS WAS SO IMPRESSED BY THE MUSIC THAT HE STUDIED IT CONTINOUSLY FOR THREE MONTHS, AND HE WAS SO ENAMORED OF IT THAT EVEN THE TASTE OF MEAT ESCAPED HIS NOTICE.

BONG

I NEVER KNEW THE STUDY OF MUSIC COULD BRING ONE TO SUCH A STATE!

景公問政孔子，孔子曰：「君君，臣臣，父父，子子。」景公曰：「善哉！信如君不君，臣不臣，父不父，子不子，雖有粟，吾豈得而食諸！」他日又復問政於孔子，孔子曰：「政在節財。」景公說，將欲以尼谿田封孔子。晏嬰進曰：「夫儒者滑稽而不可軌法；倨傲自順，不可以為下；崇喪遂哀，破產厚葬，不可以為俗；游說乞貸，不可以為國。自大賢之息，周室既衰，禮樂缺有間。今孔子盛容飾，繁登降之禮，趨詳之節，累世不能殫其學，當年不能究其禮。君欲用之以移齊俗，非所以先細民也。」後景公敬見孔

THE SPRING & AUTUMN PERIOD IN CHINA WAS A FRIGHTFULLY CHAOTIC TIME. NOT ONLY WAS DUKE ZHAO OF LU TOPPLED AND EXILED BY THE NOBLEMAN JISUN,

BUT DUKE JING OF QI WAS THE PUPPET OF ONE CHEN HUAN. AS CHEN HUAN'S POWER GREW, THE CHANCES OF HIS COMPLETELY USURPING THE THRONE GREW AS WELL.

SO DUKE JING SOUGHT ADVICE FROM CONFUCIUS ON THE PRINCIPLES OF GOVERNING. CONFUCIUS REPLIED:

KINGS SHOULD ACT LIKE KINGS; MINISTERS SHOULD ACT LIKE MINISTERS; FATHERS SHOULD ACT LIKE FATHERS; AND SONS SHOULD ACT LIKE SONS.

EXCELLENT! IF PEOPLE DON'T PLAY THEIR APPROPRIATE ROLES, THEN NO MATTER HOW MUCH FOOD THERE IS, WILL WE EVER BE ABLE TO EAT IT IN PEACE?

WHAT'S ANOTHER PRINCIPLE OF GOVERNING?

THE MOST IMPORTANT THING IN GOVERNING IS TO UTILIZE REVENUE INTELLIGENTLY AND AVOID WASTE.

I THINK I'LL ENFEOFF CONFUCIUS WITH THE NIXI FIELDS.

子，不問其禮。異日，景公止孔子曰：「奉子以季氏，吾不能。」以季孟之間待之。齊大夫欲害孔子，孔子聞之。景公曰：「吾老矣，弗能用也。」孔子遂行，反乎魯。

孔子年四十二，魯昭公卒於乾侯，定公立。定公立五年，夏，季平子卒，桓子嗣立。季桓子穿井得土缶，中若羊，問仲尼云「得狗」。仲尼曰：「以丘所聞，羊也。丘聞之，木石之怪夔、罔閬，水之怪龍、罔象，土之怪墳羊。」

29

THESE SOPHISTS TALK A GOOD TALK, SIRE, BUT THEY'RE PROUD AND DIFFICULT TO CONTROL. THEY'RE ALSO COMPLETELY UNPRODUCTIVE. ALL THEY DO IS TRAVEL AROUND SELLING THEIR IDEAS,

HOPING TO GET A GOOD POSITION AND IMPLEMENT THEIR OWN REFORMS.

DON'T LET THEM GET CONTROL OF THE GOVERNMENT.

ALL RIGHT, ALL RIGHT. WE'LL JUST FORGET HIM.

MEANWHILE, SOME HIGH-LEVEL OFFICIALS OF QI WERE ALSO PLOTTING AGAINST CONFUCIUS.

MASTER, I'VE LEARNED THAT THERE ARE PEOPLE WHO WISH TO DO YOU HARM!

OH! IS THAT RIGHT...

DUKE JING SAID TO CONFUCIUS:

I'M GETTING OLD AND SO WILL HAVE NO FURTHER USE FOR YOU.

IS THAT RIGHT...

SO CONFUCIUS LEFT QI AND RETURNED TO LU.

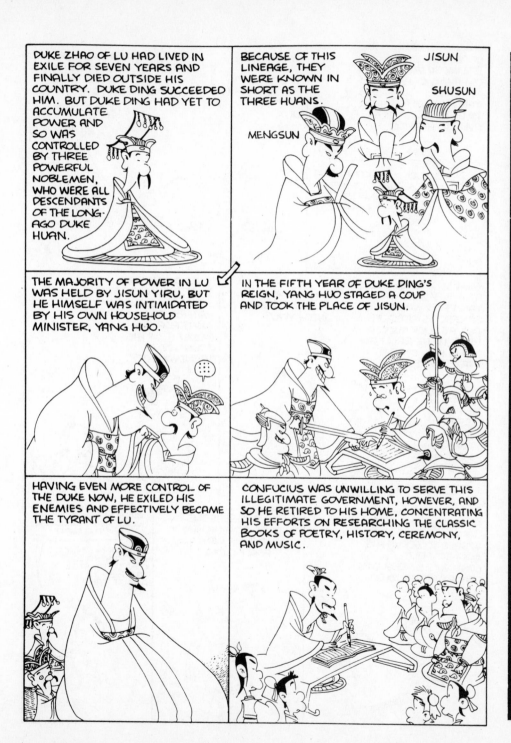

**Panel 1:** DUKE ZHAO OF LU HAD LIVED IN EXILE FOR SEVEN YEARS AND FINALLY DIED OUTSIDE HIS COUNTRY. DUKE DING SUCCEEDED HIM. BUT DUKE DING HAD YET TO ACCUMULATE POWER AND SO WAS CONTROLLED BY THREE POWERFUL NOBLEMEN, WHO WERE ALL DESCENDANTS OF THE LONG-AGO DUKE HUAN.

**Panel 2:** BECAUSE OF THIS LINEAGE, THEY WERE KNOWN IN SHORT AS THE THREE HUANS.

JISUN
SHUSUN
MENGSUN

**Panel 3:** THE MAJORITY OF POWER IN LU WAS HELD BY JISUN YIRU, BUT HE HIMSELF WAS INTIMIDATED BY HIS OWN HOUSEHOLD MINISTER, YANG HUO.

**Panel 4:** IN THE FIFTH YEAR OF DUKE DING'S REIGN, YANG HUO STAGED A COUP AND TOOK THE PLACE OF JISUN.

**Panel 5:** HAVING EVEN MORE CONTROL OF THE DUKE NOW, HE EXILED HIS ENEMIES AND EFFECTIVELY BECAME THE TYRANT OF LU.

**Panel 6:** CONFUCIUS WAS UNWILLING TO SERVE THIS ILLEGITIMATE GOVERNMENT, HOWEVER, AND SO HE RETIRED TO HIS HOME, CONCENTRATING HIS EFFORTS ON RESEARCHING THE CLASSIC BOOKS OF POETRY, HISTORY, CEREMONY, AND MUSIC.

桓子嬖臣曰仲梁懷，與陽虎有隙。陽虎欲逐懷，公山不狃止之。其秋，懷益驕，陽虎怒，囚桓子，與盟而釋之。陽虎由此益輕季氏。季氏亦僭於公室，陪臣執國政，是以魯自大夫以下皆僭離於正道。故孔子不仕，退而脩詩書禮樂，弟子彌眾，至自遠方，莫不受業焉。

定公八年，公山不狃不得意於季氏，因陽虎為亂，欲廢三桓之適，更立其庶孽陽虎素所善者，遂執季桓子。桓子詐之，得脫。定公九年，陽虎不勝，奔于齊。是時孔子年五十。

31

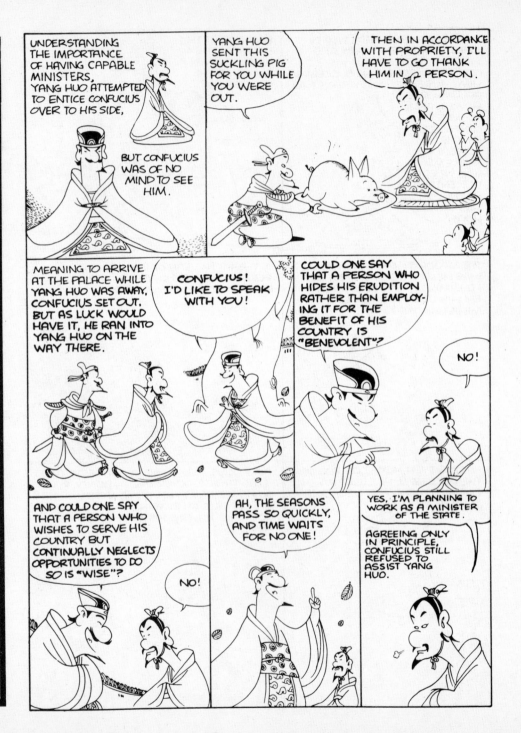

公山不狃以費畔季氏，使人召孔子。孔子循道彌久，溫溫無所試，莫能己用，曰：「蓋周文武起豐鎬而王，今費雖小，儻庶幾乎！」欲往。子路不說，止孔子。孔子曰：「夫召我者豈徒哉？如用我，其為東周乎！」然亦卒不行。

其後定公以孔子為中都宰，一年，四方皆則之。由中都宰為司空，由司空為大司寇。

定公十年春，及齊平。夏，齊大夫黎鉏言於景公曰：「魯用孔丘，其勢危齊。」乃使使告魯為好會，

UNDERSTANDING THE IMPORTANCE OF HAVING CAPABLE MINISTERS, YANG HUO ATTEMPTED TO ENTICE CONFUCIUS OVER TO HIS SIDE,

BUT CONFUCIUS WAS OF NO MIND TO SEE HIM.

YANG HUO SENT THIS SUCKLING PIG FOR YOU WHILE YOU WERE OUT.

THEN IN ACCORDANCE WITH PROPRIETY, I'LL HAVE TO GO THANK HIM IN PERSON.

MEANING TO ARRIVE AT THE PALACE WHILE YANG HUO WAS AWAY, CONFUCIUS SET OUT. BUT AS LUCK WOULD HAVE IT, HE RAN INTO YANG HUO ON THE WAY THERE.

CONFUCIUS! I'D LIKE TO SPEAK WITH YOU!

COULD ONE SAY THAT A PERSON WHO HIDES HIS ERUDITION RATHER THAN EMPLOYING IT FOR THE BENEFIT OF HIS COUNTRY IS "BENEVOLENT"?

NO!

AND COULD ONE SAY THAT A PERSON WHO WISHES TO SERVE HIS COUNTRY BUT CONTINUALLY NEGLECTS OPPORTUNITIES TO DO SO IS "WISE"?

NO!

AH, THE SEASONS PASS SO QUICKLY, AND TIME WAITS FOR NO ONE!

YES, I'M PLANNING TO WORK AS A MINISTER OF THE STATE.

AGREEING ONLY IN PRINCIPLE, CONFUCIUS STILL REFUSED TO ASSIST YANG HUO.

32

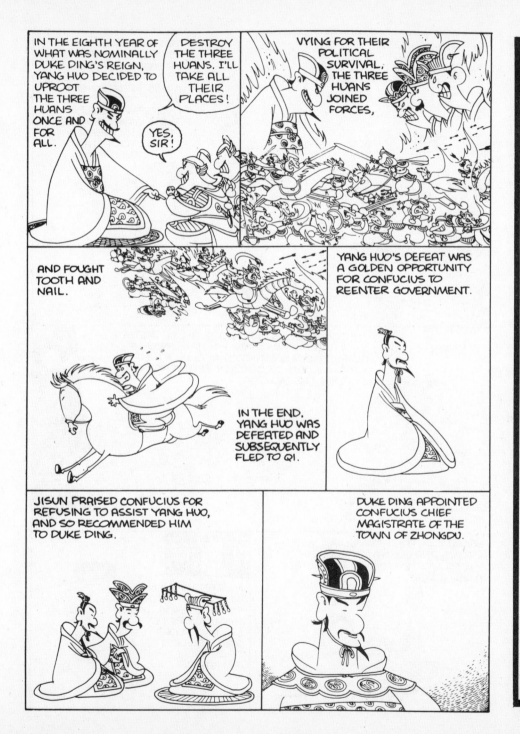

IN THE EIGHTH YEAR OF WHAT WAS NOMINALLY DUKE DING'S REIGN, YANG HUO DECIDED TO UPROOT THE THREE HUANS ONCE AND FOR ALL.

DESTROY THE THREE HUANS. I'LL TAKE ALL THEIR PLACES!

YES, SIR!

VYING FOR THEIR POLITICAL SURVIVAL, THE THREE HUANS JOINED FORCES,

AND FOUGHT TOOTH AND NAIL.

IN THE END, YANG HUO WAS DEFEATED AND SUBSEQUENTLY FLED TO QI.

YANG HUO'S DEFEAT WAS A GOLDEN OPPORTUNITY FOR CONFUCIUS TO REENTER GOVERNMENT.

JISUN PRAISED CONFUCIUS FOR REFUSING TO ASSIST YANG HUO, AND SO RECOMMENDED HIM TO DUKE DING.

DUKE DING APPOINTED CONFUCIUS CHIEF MAGISTRATE OF THE TOWN OF ZHONGDU.

會於夾谷。魯定公且以乘車好往。孔子攝相事，曰：「臣聞有文事者必有武備，有武事者必有文備。古者諸侯出疆，必具官以從。請具左右司馬。」定公曰：「諾。」具左右司馬。會齊侯夾谷，為壇位，土階三等，以會遇之禮相見，揖讓而登。獻酬之禮畢，齊有司趨而進曰：「請奏四方之樂。」景公曰：「諾。」於是旍旄羽袚矛戟劍撥鼓噪而至。孔子趨而進，歷階而登，不盡一等，舉袂而言曰：「吾兩君為好會，夷狄之樂何為於此！請命有司！」有司卻之，不去，則左右視晏子與景公。景公心怍，麾而去之。有頃，齊

33

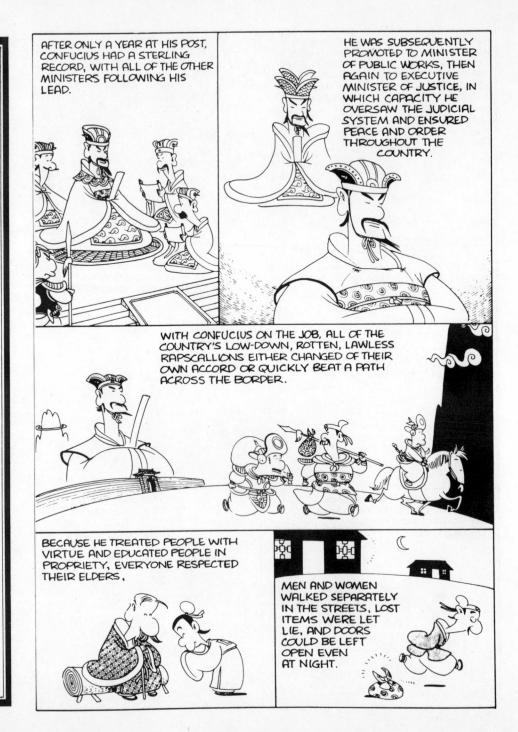

AFTER ONLY A YEAR AT HIS POST, CONFUCIUS HAD A STERLING RECORD, WITH ALL OF THE OTHER MINISTERS FOLLOWING HIS LEAD.

HE WAS SUBSEQUENTLY PROMOTED TO MINISTER OF PUBLIC WORKS, THEN AGAIN TO EXECUTIVE MINISTER OF JUSTICE, IN WHICH CAPACITY HE OVERSAW THE JUDICIAL SYSTEM AND ENSURED PEACE AND ORDER THROUGHOUT THE COUNTRY.

WITH CONFUCIUS ON THE JOB, ALL OF THE COUNTRY'S LOW-DOWN, ROTTEN, LAWLESS RAPSCALLIONS EITHER CHANGED OF THEIR OWN ACCORD OR QUICKLY BEAT A PATH ACROSS THE BORDER.

BECAUSE HE TREATED PEOPLE WITH VIRTUE AND EDUCATED PEOPLE IN PROPRIETY, EVERYONE RESPECTED THEIR ELDERS,

MEN AND WOMEN WALKED SEPARATELY IN THE STREETS, LOST ITEMS WERE LET LIE, AND DOORS COULD BE LEFT OPEN EVEN AT NIGHT.

有司趨而進曰：「請奏宮中之樂。」景公曰：「諾。」優倡侏儒為戲而前。孔子趨而進，歷階而登，不盡一等，曰：「匹夫而營惑諸侯者罪當誅！請命有司！」有司加法焉，手足異處。景公懼而動，知義不若，歸而大恐，告其羣臣曰：「魯以君子之道輔其君，而子獨以夷狄之道教寡人，使得罪於魯君，為之奈何？」有司進對曰：「君子有過則謝以質，小人有過則謝以文。君若悼之，則謝以質。」於是齊侯乃歸所侵魯之鄆、汶陽、龜陰之田以謝過。

34

IN THE TENTH YEAR OF DUKE DING'S REIGN, THE DUKE ATTEMPTED TO RECONCILE WITH QI, AND HEARING THIS, A NOBLEMAN OF QI WARNED QI'S DUKE JING:

LU HAS EMPLOYED CONFUCIUS, WHO HAS GOVERNED EXTREMELY WELL. AS LU GROWS STRONGER, THEY ARE BOUND TO BE A THREAT TO US.

CONFUCIUS MAY UNDERSTAND PROPRIETY, BUT HE IS A COWARD AT HEART. AFTER THE NEGOTIATIONS, I SUGGEST YOU USE THE BARBARIAN PERFORMERS TO TAKE THE DUKE PRISONER. CONFUCIUS WILL BE HELPLESS.

PERFECT! SEND AN EMISSARY TO ARRANGE TREATY NEGOTIATIONS WITH LU.

YES, SIRE!

EMISSARY

QI'S DUKE JING SENT AN EMISSARY TO ARRANGE A TREATY SUMMIT WITH US IN JIAGU.

WONDERFUL. ARRANGE FOR A SMALL DELEGATION TO LEAVE FOR JIAGU IMMEDIATELY.

WAIT!

定公十三年夏，孔子言於定公曰：「臣無藏甲，大夫毋百雉之城。」使仲由為季氏宰，將墮三都。於是叔孫氏先墮郈。季氏將墮費，公山不狃、叔孫輒率費人襲魯。公與三子入于季氏之宮，登武子之臺。費人攻之，弗克，入及公側。孔子命申句須、樂頎下伐之，費人北。國人追之，敗諸姑蔑。二子奔齊，遂墮費。將墮成，公斂處父謂孟孫曰：「墮成，齊人必至于北門。且成，孟氏之保鄣，無成是無孟氏也。我將弗墮。」十二月，公圍成，弗克。

I'VE HEARD THAT FOR DIPLOMATIC AFFAIRS, THERE MUST ALSO BE MILITARY READINESS, JUST AS FOR MILITARY AFFAIRS, THERE MUST ALSO BE DIPLOMATIC READINESS.

WHENEVER NOBLEMEN OF THE PAST CROSSED THEIR COUNTRY'S BORDERS, THEY WERE ALWAYS SURE TO GO WITH A MILITARY ACCOMPANIMENT IN ADDITION TO THEIR DIPLOMATIC DELEGATION. I SUGGEST YOU DO LIKEWISE.

FINE.

SO THE DUKE SET OUT FOR JIAGU WITH CONFUCIUS AND A FULL MILITARY COMPLEMENT.

MEETING AT THE APPOINTED PLACE, THE TWO MONARCHS BEGAN BY EXCHANGING FORMALITIES.

定公十四年，孔子年五十六，由大司寇行攝相事，有喜色。門人曰：「聞君子禍至不懼，福至不喜。」孔子曰：「有是言也。不曰『樂其以貴下人』乎？」於是誅魯大夫亂政者少正卯。與聞國政三月，粥羔豚者弗飾賈；男女行者別於塗；塗不拾遺；四方之客至乎邑者不求有司，皆予之以歸。齊人聞而懼，曰：「孔子為政必霸，霸則吾地近焉，我之為先并矣。盍致地焉？」黎鉏曰：「請先嘗沮之；沮之而不可則致地，庸遲乎！」於是選齊國中女子好者八十人，皆衣文衣而舞康樂，文馬三十駟，

36

FOLLOWING THE FORMALITIES, THE TWO SIDES DREW UP A TREATY TOGETHER.

WHEN THE DUKE OF QI ADDED AN UNEXPECTED PROVISION...

IN THE EVENT THAT QI CROSS ITS BORDERS TO WAGE WAR, LU SHALL SEND MILITARY ASSISTANCE IN THE FORM OF THREE HUNDRED MANNED CHARIOTS.

QI-LU ALLIANCE

NOT WANTING TO BE TAKEN ADVANTAGE OF, CONFUCIUS ADDED A PROVISION OF HIS OWN...

ALL THE QI-OCCUPIED LAND NORTH OF THE WEN RIVER SHALL BE RETURNED TO LU.

SCOUNDREL!

QI-LU ALLIANCE

RIGHT!

DO IT NOW, SIRE.

BEGIN THE FESTIVITIES!

YA, YA, YA, YA, YA

遺魯君。陳女樂文馬於魯城南高門外。季桓子微服往觀再三，將受，乃語魯君為周道游，往觀終日，怠於政事。子路曰：「夫子可以行矣。」孔子曰：「魯今且郊，如致膰乎大夫，則吾猶可以止。」桓子卒受齊女樂，三日不聽政；郊，又不致膰俎於大夫。孔子遂行，宿乎屯。而師己送，曰：「夫子則非罪。」孔子曰：「吾歌可夫？」歌曰：「彼婦之口，可以出走；彼婦之謁，可以死敗。蓋優哉游哉，維以卒歲！」師己反，桓子曰：「孔子亦何言？」師己以實告。桓子喟然歎曰：「夫子罪我以羣婢故也夫！」

37

YAI YAI YAI YAI

LAI

AHH!

HOLD IT!

TWO SOVEREIGNS CAME HERE TO NEGOTIATE AN ALLIANCE; WHAT NEED IS THERE FOR THIS KIND OF BARBARIAN ENTERTAINMENT? PLEASE ASK THEM TO LEAVE!

WITHDRAW!

孔子遂適衛，主於子路妻兄顏濁鄒家。衛靈公問孔子：「居魯得祿幾何？」對曰：「奉粟六萬。」衛人亦致粟六萬。居頃之，或譖孔子於衛靈公。靈公使公孫余假一出一入。孔子恐獲罪焉，居十月，去衛。

將適陳，過匡，顏刻為僕，以其策指之曰：「昔吾入此，由彼缺也。」匡人聞之，以為魯之陽虎。陽虎嘗暴匡人；匡人於是遂止孔子。孔子狀類陽虎，拘焉五日。顏淵後，子曰：「吾以汝為死矣。」顏淵曰：「子在，回何敢死！」匡人拘孔子益急，弟子懼。孔子曰：「文王既沒，文不在茲乎？天之將喪斯文也

38

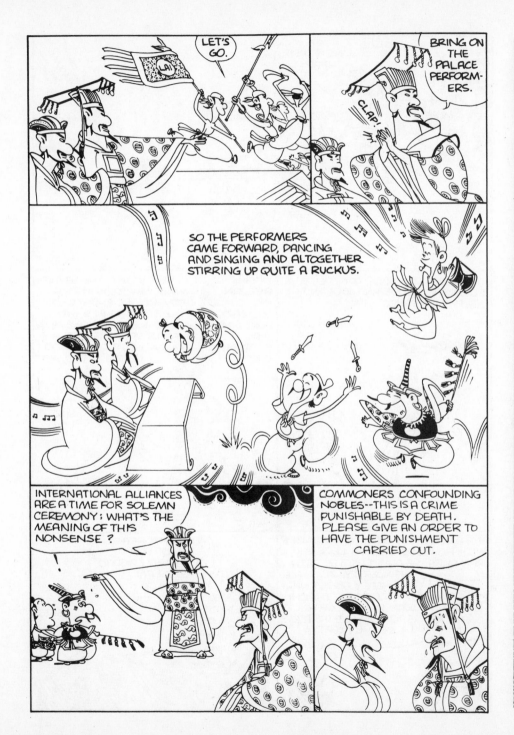

LET'S GO.

BRING ON THE PALACE PERFORMERS.

CLAP!

SO THE PERFORMERS CAME FORWARD, DANCING AND SINGING AND ALTOGETHER STIRRING UP QUITE A RUCKUS.

INTERNATIONAL ALLIANCES ARE A TIME FOR SOLEMN CEREMONY; WHAT'S THE MEANING OF THIS NONSENSE?

COMMONERS CONFOUNDING NOBLES--THIS IS A CRIME PUNISHABLE BY DEATH. PLEASE GIVE AN ORDER TO HAVE THE PUNISHMENT CARRIED OUT.

，後死者不得與于斯文也。天之未喪斯文也，匡人其如予何！」孔子使從者為甯武子臣於衞，然後得去。

去即過蒲。月餘，反乎衞，主蘧伯玉家。靈公夫人有南子者，使人謂孔子曰：「四方之君子不辱欲與寡君為兄弟者，必見寡小君。寡小君願見。」孔子辭謝，不得已而見之。夫人在絺帷中。孔子入門，北面稽首。夫人自帷中再拜，環珮玉聲璆然。孔子曰：「吾鄉為弗見，見之禮答焉。」子路不說。孔子矢之曰：「予所不者，天厭之！天厭之！」居衞月餘，靈公與夫人同車，宦者雍渠參乘，出，使孔子為次乘，招

OFF WITH THEIR HEADS!

AHHH!

DUKE JING OBSERVED CONFUCIUS' SEVERE ATTITUDE AND COULDN'T HELP BUT RESPECT HIM.

UPON RETURNING TO HIS COUNTRY, DUKE JING WAS EXTREMELY UPSET...

CONFUCIUS USES THE GENTLEMAN'S WAY TO ASSIST HIS SOVEREIGN. AND YOU USE THE BARBARIAN'S WAY TO EMBARRASS ME. WE MADE FOOLS OF OURSELVES, AND NOW WHAT CAN WE DO ABOUT IT?

WOULD THAT I DIE, SIRE?

IF A GENTLEMAN ERRS, HE APOLOGIZES WITH HIS DEEDS. WHEN A LESSER MAN ERRS, HE COMPENSATES WITH INSINCERITY. IF YOU FEEL UNEASY ABOUT WHAT HAPPENED, THE ONLY WAY TO MAKE UP FOR IT IS TO OBSERVE THE TERMS OF THE TREATY.

ALL RIGHT! RETURN ALL OF OUR OCCUPIED LAND TO LU AS AN APOLOGY.

YES, SIRE.

搖市過之。孔子曰：「吾未見好德如好色者也。」於是醜之，去衛，過曹。是歲，魯定公卒。

孔子去曹適宋，與弟子習禮大樹下。宋司馬桓魋欲殺孔子，拔其樹。孔子去。弟子曰：「可以速矣。」

孔子曰：「天生德於予，桓魋其如予何！」

孔子適鄭，與弟子相失，孔子獨立郭東門。鄭人或謂子貢曰：「東門有人，其顙似堯，其項類皋陶，其

肩類子產，然自要以下不及禹三寸，纍纍若喪家之狗。」子貢以實告孔子。孔子欣然笑曰：「形狀，末也

40

Panel 1: IN THE SUMMER OF LU DUKE DING'S TWELFTH YEAR ON THE THRONE:

I'D LIKE TO RETURN THE MILITARY POWER OF THE NOBLEMEN TO THE CENTRAL GOVERNMENT AND SO PROPOSE THAT THE THREE HUANS TEAR DOWN THE WALLS OF THEIR CITIES.

ALL RIGHT.

Panel 2: I PLAN ON TEARING DOWN THE WALLS OF YOUR THREE CITIES TO PREVENT ANOTHER YANG HUO INCIDENT FROM HAPPENING.

Panel 3: THAT'S A GOOD IDEA. THAT WAY OUR HOUSEHOLD MINISTERS WOULDN'T BE ABLE TO USE OUR CITIES AS BASES FOR REVOLT.

Panel 4: SHUSUN WAS THE FIRST TO DESTROY HIS CITY WALL.

Panel 5: GONGSHAN BUNIU, I ORDER YOU TO REMOVE YOUR TROOPS FROM THE CITY WALL, AS OUR CITY OF BI SHALL NO LONGER HAVE A WALL!

Panel 6: THAT DASTARDLY JISUN IS GOING TO DESTROY OUR BASE OF OPERATIONS. WHAT SHOULD WE DO?

IT FIGURES! HE'S AFRAID WE'LL TAKE OVER...

而謂似喪家之狗，然哉！然哉！」

孔子遂至陳，主於司城貞子家。歲餘，吳王夫差伐陳，取三邑而去。趙鞅伐朝歌。楚圍蔡，蔡遷于吳，吳敗越王句踐會稽。

有隼集于陳廷而死，楛矢貫之，石砮，矢長尺有咫。陳湣公使使問仲尼。仲尼曰：「隼來遠矣，此肅慎之矢也。昔武王克商，通道九夷百蠻，使各以其方賄來貢，使無忘職業。於是肅慎貢楛矢石砮，長尺有

41

THEN WE'LL FINISH THIS ONCE AND FOR ALL! MUSTER THE TROOPS!

TROUBLE, SIRE! GONGSHAN BUNIU HAS CALLED HIS TROOPS TO BATTLE AND IS TAKING OVER...

DUKE DING AND THE THREE HUANS TOOK REFUGE IN JISUN'S PALACE...

SHEN JUXU AND YUE QI, TAKE YOUR TROOPS AND SUPPRESS THEM.

THE BI ARMY BEGAN TO RETREAT AND WAS THOROUGHLY DEFEATED AT GUMIE, BUT GONGSHAN BUNIU AND HIS REMAINING MEN ESCAPED TO QI.

尺。先王欲昭其令德，以肅慎矢分大姬，配虞胡公而封諸陳。分同姓以珍玉，展親；分異姓以遠方職，使無忘服。故分陳以肅慎矢。」試求之故府，果得之。

孔子居陳三歲，會晉楚爭彊，更伐陳，及吳侵陳，陳常被寇。孔子曰：「歸與歸與！吾黨之小子狂簡，進取不忘其初。」於是孔子去陳。

過蒲，會公叔氏以蒲畔，蒲人止孔子。弟子有公良孺者，以私車五乘從孔子。其為人長賢，有勇力，

42

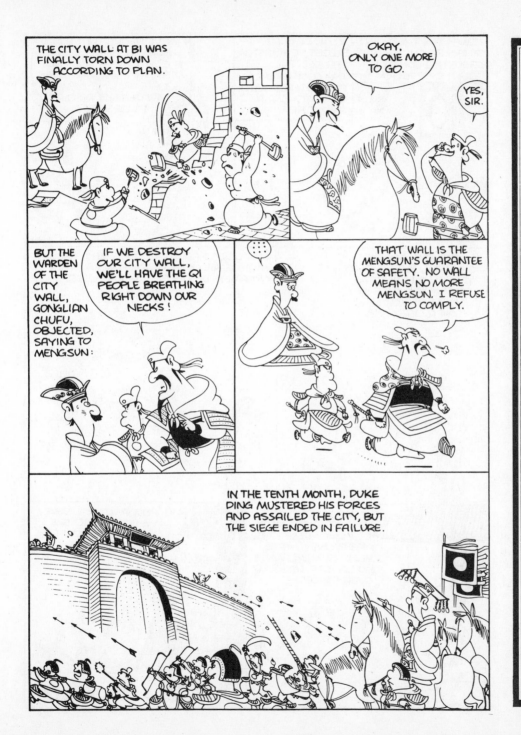

THE CITY WALL AT BI WAS FINALLY TORN DOWN ACCORDING TO PLAN.

OKAY, ONLY ONE MORE TO GO.

YES, SIR.

BUT THE WARDEN OF THE CITY WALL, GONGLIAN CHUFU, OBJECTED, SAYING TO MENGSUN:

IF WE DESTROY OUR CITY WALL, WE'LL HAVE THE QI PEOPLE BREATHING RIGHT DOWN OUR NECKS!

THAT WALL IS THE MENGSUN'S GUARANTEE OF SAFETY. NO WALL MEANS NO MORE MENGSUN. I REFUSE TO COMPLY.

IN THE TENTH MONTH, DUKE DING MUSTERED HIS FORCES AND ASSAILED THE CITY, BUT THE SIEGE ENDED IN FAILURE.

謂曰：「吾昔從夫子遇難於匡，今又遇難於此，命也已。吾與夫子再罹難，寧鬥而死。」鬥甚疾。蒲人懼，謂孔子曰：「苟毋適衞，吾出子。」與之盟，出孔子東門。孔子遂適衞。子貢曰：「盟可負邪？」孔子曰：「要盟也，神不聽。」

衞靈公聞孔子來，喜，郊迎。問曰：「蒲可伐乎？」對曰：「可。」靈公曰：「吾大夫以為不可。今蒲，衞之所以待晉楚也，以衞伐之，無乃不可乎？」孔子曰：「其男子有死之志，婦人有保西河之志。吾

所伐者不過四五人。」靈公不伐蒲。

靈公老，怠於政，不用孔子。趙簡子攻范、中行，伐中牟。佛肸為中牟宰。佛肸畔，使人召孔子。孔子欲往。子路曰：「由聞諸夫子，『其身親為不善者，君子不入也』。今佛肸親以中牟畔，子欲往，如之何？」孔子曰：「有是言也。不曰堅乎，磨而不磷；不曰白乎，涅而不淄。我豈匏瓜也哉，焉能繫而不食？」

靈公曰：「善。」然不伐蒲。孔子行。「苟有用我者，其月而已，三年有成。」孔子喟然歎曰：

IT WAS THE THIRTEENTH YEAR OF DUKE DING'S REIGN, WHEN AS EXECUTIVE MINISTER OF JUSTICE CONFUCIUS ATTENDED THE COUNTRY'S POLICY-MAKING CONFERENCE AND ENTERED WITH A GLOATING AIR ABOUT HIM.

I'VE HEARD THAT WHEN DISASTER IS IMMINENT, A GENTLEMAN DOES NOT DISPLAY FEAR, AND WHEN GOOD FORTUNE COMES, HE DOES NOT DISPLAY PLEASURE.

YES, SOMEONE DID SAY THAT, BUT HAVEN'T YOU ALSO HEARD THE SAYING "REJOICE IN YOUR POSITION OVER OTHERS"?

CONFUCIUS HAD SHAOZHENG MAO, THE HIGH-LEVEL OFFICIAL RESPONSIBLE FOR CREATING UNREST IN LU, EXECUTED.

WITH CONFUCIUS PARTICIPATING IN POLICY DECISIONS, AFTER ONLY THREE MONTHS, MERCHANTS NO LONGER HAGGLED OVER PRICES.

NO SECOND PRICE

AND VISITORS WERE WELCOMED TO THE COUNTRY WITH OPEN ARMS.

BORDER

WELCOME TO LU, NO VISA REQUIRED.

44

WHEN QI HEARD OF THE SUCCESS OF THE LU GOVERNMENT, THEY BEGAN TO WORRY...

IF CONFUCIUS CONTINUES TO GOVERN LU, THEY WILL ONLY GET STRONGER AND EVENTUALLY START COMPETING FOR HEGEMONY. AND SINCE QI IS THEIR NEAREST NEIGHBOR, WE'LL BE THE FIRST TO BE SWALLOWED UP...

OR WE COULD THINK OF A WAY TO SABOTAGE THEIR REFORMS. I SAY WE SEND SOME BEAUTIFUL WOMEN TO THEIR SOVEREIGN AS A DISTRACTION.

OKAY! THAT'S WHAT WE'LL DO.

SO QI SENT EIGHTY WOMEN AND ONE HUNDRED TWENTY HORSES TO LU...

DUKE JING SENT US SOME FEMALE ENTERTAINMENT AND FINE HORSES. THEY'RE WAITING OUTSIDE THE SOUTHERN GATE RIGHT NOW.

LET'S GO TAKE A LOOK.

孔子擊磬。有荷蕢而過門者，曰：「有心哉，擊磬乎！莫己知也夫而已矣！

孔子學鼓琴師襄子，十日不進。師襄子曰：「可以益矣。」

孔子曰：「已習其數，可以益矣。」有閒，曰：「丘未得其志也。」孔子曰：「已習其志，可以益矣

。」孔子曰：「丘未得其為人也。」有閒，有所穆然深思焉，有所怡然高望而遠志焉。曰：「丘得其為人

，黯然而黑，幾然而長，眼如望羊，如王四國，非文王其誰能為此也！」師襄子辟席再拜，曰：「師蓋云

有閒，曰：「可以益矣。」孔子曰：「丘已習其曲矣，未得其數也。

硜硜乎，莫己知也夫而已矣！」

45

DUKE DING AND JISUN SI SPENT THREE DAYS ENRAPTURED BY THE WOMEN, OBLIVIOUS TO THE AFFAIRS OF THE COUNTRY.

IN ADDITION TO THIS, THE PROPER CEREMONY WAS NOT FOLLOWED AT THE TIME OF THE SPRING SACRIFICE IN THAT THE RIGHTFUL PORTIONS OF SACRIFICIAL MEAT WERE NOT ALLOTTED TO THE OFFICIALS.

MASTER, I THINK WE SHOULD LEAVE.

YES.

YANG HUO AND HIS BAND HAVE BEEN COMPLETELY WIPED OUT, AND JISUN'S POSITION FIRMLY ESTABLISHED. I FEAR THEY'LL NO LONGER SEE A NEED FOR ME, NOT TO MENTION THAT THE DUKE HAS LOST ALL OF HIS REAL AUTHORITY...

LET'S GO.

SO CONFUCIUS RESIGNED HIS POST AS MINISTER OF JUSTICE, DEPARTING LU FOR THE STATE OF WEI...

文王操也。」

孔子既不得用於衛，將西見趙簡子。至於河而聞竇鳴犢、舜華之死也，臨河而歎曰：「美哉水，洋洋乎！丘之不濟此，命也夫！」子貢趨而進曰：「敢問何謂也？」孔子曰：「竇鳴犢、舜華，晉國之賢大夫也。趙簡子未得志之時，須此兩人而后從政；及其已得志，殺之乃從政。丘聞之也，刳胎殺夭則麒麟不至郊，竭澤涸漁則蛟龍不合陰陽，覆巢毀卵則鳳皇不翔。何則？君子諱傷其類也。夫鳥獸之於不義也尚知辟

46

UPON ARRIVAL IN THE CAPITAL OF WEI, CONFUCIUS NOTICED THE FLOURISHING POPULATION...

WOW, LOOK AT ALL THE PEOPLE HERE...

MASTER, WHEN THE GOAL OF POPULATION GROWTH HAS BEEN ACHIEVED, WHAT SHOULD BE DONE NEXT?

MAKE THEM PROSPEROUS.

AND AFTER THEY ARE PROSPEROUS, WHAT NEXT?

EDUCATE THEM.

CONFUCIUS REMAINED IN WEI, STAYING AT THE HOME OF YAN SHUZOU, THE UNCLE OF HIS DISCIPLE ZHONG YOU.

之，而況乎丘哉！」乃還息乎陬鄉，作為陬操以哀之。而反乎衛，入主蘧伯玉家。

他日，靈公問兵陳。孔子曰：「俎豆之事則嘗聞之，軍旅之事未之學也。」明日，與孔子語，見蜚鴈，仰視之，色不在孔子。孔子遂行，復如陳。

夏，衛靈公卒，立孫輒，是為衛出公。六月，趙鞅內太子蒯瞶于戚。陽虎使太子絻，八人衰絰，偽自衛迎者，哭而入，遂居焉。冬，蔡遷于州來。是歲魯哀公三年，而孔子年六十矣。齊助衛圍戚，以衛太子

47

WEI'S DUKE LING INVITED CONFUCIUS TO THE PALACE.

WHAT WAS YOUR SALARY IN LU?

I WAS PAID SIXTY THOUSAND GRAINS OF MILLET.

I'LL MATCH WHAT YOU WERE PAID IN LU.

THANK YOU.

SHORTLY, PEOPLE BEGAN MALIGNING CONFUCIUS IN THE PRESENCE OF THE DUKE...

AS A RESULT, DUKE LING STATIONED SOLDIERS AT CONFUCIUS' RESIDENCE TO HARASS HIM.

FEARING THE WORST, CONFUCIUS REMAINED FOR ONLY TEN MONTHS, THEN SET OUT FOR THE STATE OF CHEN.

蒯瞶在故也。

夏，魯桓釐廟燔，南宮敬叔救火。孔子在陳，聞之，曰：「災必於桓釐廟乎？」已而果然。

秋，季桓子病，輦而見魯城，喟然歎曰：「昔此國幾興矣，以吾獲罪於孔子，故不興也。」顧謂其嗣康子曰：「我即死，若必相魯；相魯，必召仲尼。」後數日，桓子卒，康子代立。已葬，欲召仲尼。公之魚曰：「昔吾先君用之不終，終為諸侯笑。今又用之，不能終，是再為諸侯笑。」康子曰：「則誰召而可

48

**Panel 1:** YAN KE WAS DRIVING CONFUCIUS' CARRIAGE WHEN THEY PASSED THROUGH THE ZHENG CITY OF KUANG. NOTICING A HOLE IN THE WALL (BY WAY OF WHICH THE CITY HAD BEEN ATTACKED BEFORE...)

ONCE WHEN I CAME HERE, I ENTERED THROUGH THAT HOLE IN THE WALL.

**Panel 2:** OH NO! YANG HUO'S BACK! RUN FOR COVER! YANG HUO'S BACK!

**Panel 3:** YANG HUO HAD TERRORIZED KUANG IN THE PAST, AND AS CONFUCIUS RESEMBLED YANG HUO IN APPEARANCE, THE PEOPLE OF KUANG ENCIRCLED HIM, THREATENING VENGEANCE...

**Panel 4:** THE ANCIENT ZHOU KING WEN, FOUNDER OF OUR CULTURE, IS LONG DEAD, SO DON'T THE TRADITIONS OF OUR CULTURE REST ON MY SHOULDERS? IF HEAVEN WANTS TO DESTROY THIS CULTURE, THEN IT WILL LET ME DIE, AND THE CULTURE WILL DIE WITH ME...

**Panel 5:** BUT IF HEAVEN DOESN'T WANT TO DESTROY THIS CULTURE, WHAT CAN THE KUANG PEOPLE DO TO ME?

?」曰：「必召冉求。」於是使召冉求。冉求將行，孔子曰：「魯人召求，非小用之，將大用之也。」子贛知孔子思歸，送冉求，因誠曰「即用，以孔子為招」云。

是日，孔子曰：「歸乎歸乎！吾黨之小子狂簡，斐然成章，吾不知所以裁之，

冉求既去，明年，孔子自陳遷于蔡。蔡昭公將如吳，吳召之也。前昭公欺其臣遷州來，後將往，大夫

懼復遷，公孫翻射殺昭公。楚侵蔡。秋，齊景公卒。

49

IN THE MIDST OF THE CONFUSION, CONFUCIUS' PRIZED PUPIL, YAN HUI, BECAME LOST, AND UPON HIS RETURN...

MASTER!

I THOUGHT SOMETHING HAD HAPPENED TO YOU!

WHILE YOU ARE STILL HERE, MASTER, HOW COULD I DARE GO OFF AND DIE?

AFTER KEEPING CONFUCIUS ENCIRCLED FOR FIVE DAYS, THE PEOPLE OF KUANG FINALLY DISPERSED...

MY APOLOGIES! WE MISTOOK YOU FOR YANG HUO.

SO CONFUCIUS LEFT KUANG AND HEADED FOR PU, WHERE HE STAYED FOR ONE MONTH, THEN RETURNED TO THE WEI CAPITAL.

THERE, HE STAYED AT THE HOME OF A WELL-REGARDED HIGH-LEVEL OFFICIAL, QU BOYU.

明年，孔子自蔡如葉。葉公問政，孔子曰：「政在來遠附邇。」他日，葉公問孔子於子路，子路不對。孔子聞之，曰：「由，爾何不對曰『其為人也，學道不倦，誨人不厭，發憤忘食，樂以忘憂，不知老之將至』云爾。」

去葉，反于蔡。長沮、桀溺耦而耕，孔子以為隱者，使子路問津焉。長沮曰：「彼執輿者為誰？」子路曰：「為孔丘。」曰：「是魯孔丘與？」曰：「然。」曰：「是知津矣。」桀溺謂子路曰：「子為誰？」

50

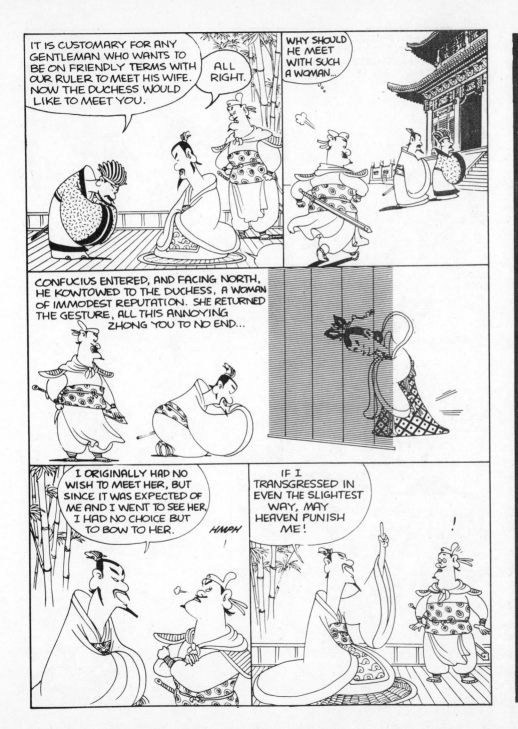

Panel 1: IT IS CUSTOMARY FOR ANY GENTLEMAN WHO WANTS TO BE ON FRIENDLY TERMS WITH OUR RULER TO MEET HIS WIFE. NOW THE DUCHESS WOULD LIKE TO MEET YOU.

ALL RIGHT.

Panel 2: WHY SHOULD HE MEET WITH SUCH A WOMAN...

Panel 3: CONFUCIUS ENTERED, AND FACING NORTH, HE KOWTOWED TO THE DUCHESS, A WOMAN OF IMMODEST REPUTATION. SHE RETURNED THE GESTURE, ALL THIS ANNOYING ZHONG YOU TO NO END...

Panel 4: I ORIGINALLY HAD NO WISH TO MEET HER, BUT SINCE IT WAS EXPECTED OF ME AND I WENT TO SEE HER, I HAD NO CHOICE BUT TO BOW TO HER.

HMPH!

Panel 5: IF I TRANSGRESSED IN EVEN THE SLIGHTEST WAY, MAY HEAVEN PUNISH ME!

!

曰：「為仲由。」曰：「子，孔丘之徒與？」曰：「然。」桀溺曰：「悠悠者天下皆是也，而誰以易之？且與其從辟人之士，豈若從辟世之士哉！」耰而不輟。子路以告孔子，孔子憮然曰：「鳥獸不可與同羣，天下有道，丘不與易也。」

他日，子路行，遇荷蓧丈人，曰：「子見夫子乎？」丈人曰：「四體不勤，五穀不分，孰為夫子！」植其杖而芸。子路以告，孔子曰：「隱者也。」復往，則亡。

51

孔子遷于蔡三歲，吳伐陳。楚救陳，軍于城父。聞孔子在陳蔡之間，楚使人聘孔子。孔子將往拜禮，

陳蔡大夫謀曰：「孔子賢者，所刺譏皆中諸侯之疾。今者久留陳蔡之間，諸大夫所設行皆非仲尼之意。今楚，大國也，來聘孔子。孔子用於楚，則陳蔡用事大夫危矣。」於是乃相與發徒役圍孔子於野。不得行，絕糧。從者病，莫能興。孔子講誦弦歌不衰。子路愠見曰：「君子亦有窮乎？」孔子曰：「君子固窮，小人窮斯濫矣。」

OVER A MONTH PASSED, AND ONE DAY DUKE LING AND HIS WIFE WERE RIDING THROUGH THE CITY WITH CONFUCIUS SECOND IN THE PROCESSION.

WEI

WOW, LOOK AT HER!

GORGEOUS!

BEAUTIFUL!

I'VE NEVER SEEN ANYONE AS INTERESTED IN THE BEAUTY OF VIRTUE AS THEY ARE IN THE BEAUTY OF A WOMAN.

FEELING DISAPPOINTED ABOUT EVERYTHING IN WEI, CONFUCIUS DEPARTED AND SET OUT FOR THE STATE OF CAO.

THAT SAME YEAR, DUKE DING OF LU PASSED AWAY.

CONFUCIUS ENDED UP LEAVING CAO AND TRAVELED TO THE STATE OF SONG WHERE THE MINISTER OF WAR, HUAN TUI, WISHED TO DO HIM HARM...

GET OUT OF HERE, CONFUCIUS!

OR YOU'LL END UP LIKE THIS TREE!

MASTER, LET'S GET OUT OF HERE...

HEAVEN ENDOWED ME WITH A MISSION OF VIRTUE, SO WHAT CAN HUAN TUI DO TO ME?!

子貢色作。孔子曰：「賜，爾以予為多學而識之者與？」曰：「然。非與？」孔子曰：「非也。予一以貫之。」

孔子知弟子有慍心，乃召子路而問曰：「詩云『匪兕匪虎，率彼曠野』。吾道非邪？吾何為於此？」

子路曰：「意者吾未仁邪？人之不我信也。意者吾未知邪？人之不我行也。」孔子曰：「有是乎！由，譬使知者而必行，安有王子比干？」

使仁者而必信，安有伯夷、叔齊？

53

子路出，子貢入見。孔子曰：「賜，詩云『匪兕匪虎，率彼曠野』。吾道非邪？吾何為於此？」子貢曰：「夫子之道至大也，故天下莫能容夫子。夫子蓋少貶焉？」孔子曰：「賜，良農能稼而不能為穡，良工能巧而不能為順。君子能脩其道，綱而紀之，統而理之，而不能為容。今爾不脩爾道而求為容。賜，而志不遠矣！」

子貢出，顏回入見。孔子曰：「回，詩云『匪兕匪虎，率彼曠野』。吾道非邪？吾何為於此？」顏回

| Panel | Text |
|---|---|

WITH NO OTHER CHOICE, CONFUCIUS DEPARTED AND SET OUT FOR THE STATE OF ZHENG, BUT ONCE THERE, HE BECAME SEPARATED FROM HIS DISCIPLES...

AT THE NORTH GATE, THERE'S A MAN WHO HAS A FOREHEAD LIKE KING YAO OF TANG; A NECK LIKE GAO YAO, THE GREAT MINISTER UNDER KING SHUN OF YU; SHOULDERS LIKE THE GREAT STATESMAN ZICHAN; AND A LOWER BODY LIKE THE GIANT-KING YU, ONLY SHORTER.

HE LOOKS DEJECTED AND ALL OUT OF SORTS, LIKE A DOG THAT'S LOST ITS WAY HOME.

MASTER!

I DON'T DESERVE TO BE COMPARED TO GREAT MEN LIKE THAT,

BUT HE WAS RIGHT ABOUT ME BEING LIKE A DOG THAT'S LOST ITS WAY HOME. NO DOUBT ABOUT THAT! NO DOUBT ABOUT THAT!

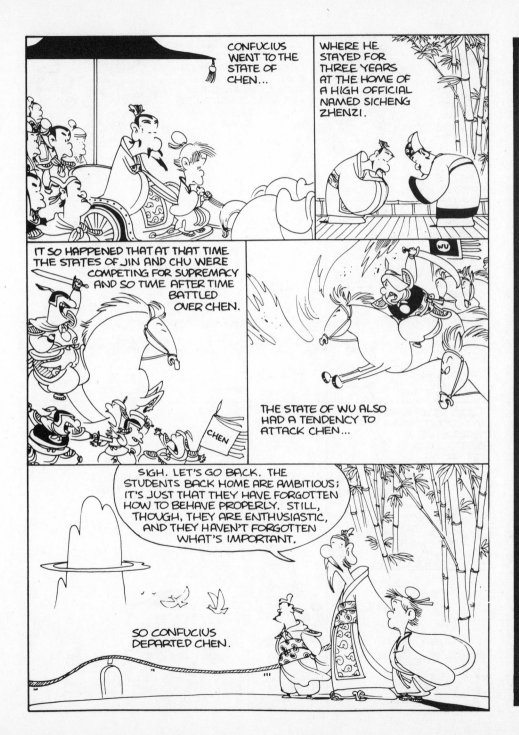

CONFUCIUS WENT TO THE STATE OF CHEN...

WHERE HE STAYED FOR THREE YEARS AT THE HOME OF A HIGH OFFICIAL NAMED SICHENG ZHENZI.

IT SO HAPPENED THAT AT THAT TIME THE STATES OF JIN AND CHU WERE COMPETING FOR SUPREMACY AND SO TIME AFTER TIME BATTLED OVER CHEN.

THE STATE OF WU ALSO HAD A TENDENCY TO ATTACK CHEN...

SIGH. LET'S GO BACK. THE STUDENTS BACK HOME ARE AMBITIOUS; IT'S JUST THAT THEY HAVE FORGOTTEN HOW TO BEHAVE PROPERLY. STILL, THOUGH, THEY ARE ENTHUSIASTIC, AND THEY HAVEN'T FORGOTTEN WHAT'S IMPORTANT.

SO CONFUCIUS DEPARTED CHEN.

日：「夫子之道至大，故天下莫能容。雖然，夫子推而行之，不容何病，不容然後見君子！夫道之不脩也，是吾醜也。夫道既已大脩而不用，是有國者之醜也。不容何病，不容然後見君子！」於是使子貢至楚。楚昭王興師迎孔子，然後得免。

昭王將以書社地七百里封孔子。楚令尹子西曰：「王之使使諸侯有如子貢者乎？」曰：「無有。」「王之輔相有如顏回者乎？」曰：「無有。」「王之將率有如子路者乎？」曰：「無有。」「王之官尹有如

「有是哉顏氏之子！使爾多財，吾為爾宰。」

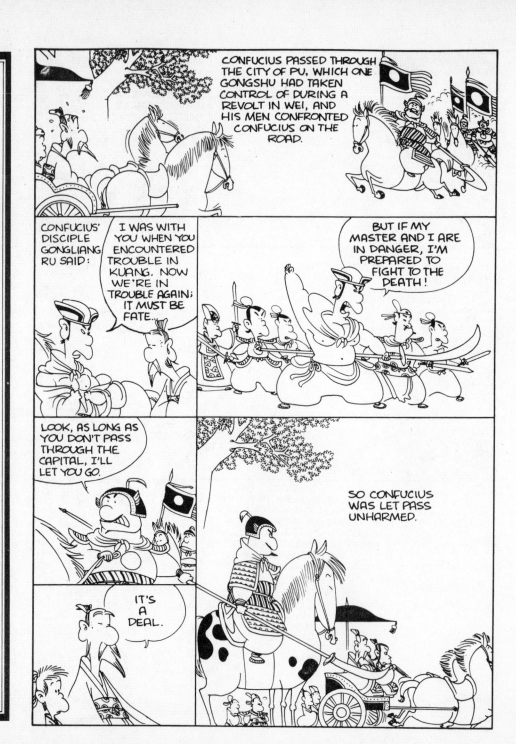

CONFUCIUS PASSED THROUGH THE CITY OF PU, WHICH ONE GONGSHU HAD TAKEN CONTROL OF DURING A REVOLT IN WEI, AND HIS MEN CONFRONTED CONFUCIUS ON THE ROAD.

CONFUCIUS' DISCIPLE GONGLIANG RU SAID:

I WAS WITH YOU WHEN YOU ENCOUNTERED TROUBLE IN KUANG. NOW WE'RE IN TROUBLE AGAIN; IT MUST BE FATE...

BUT IF MY MASTER AND I ARE IN DANGER, I'M PREPARED TO FIGHT TO THE DEATH!

LOOK, AS LONG AS YOU DON'T PASS THROUGH THE CAPITAL, I'LL LET YOU GO.

SO CONFUCIUS WAS LET PASS UNHARMED.

IT'S A DEAL.

宰予者乎?」曰:「無有。」「且楚之祖封於周,號為子男五十里。今孔丘述三五之法,明周召之業,王

若用之,則楚安得世世堂堂方數千里乎?夫文王在豐,武王在鎬,百里之君卒王天下。今孔丘得據土壤,

賢弟子為佐,非楚之福也。」昭王乃止。其秋,楚昭王卒于城父。

楚狂接輿歌而過孔子,曰:「鳳兮鳳兮,何德之衰!往者不可諫兮,來者猶可追也!已而已而,今之

從政者殆而!」孔子下,欲與之言。趨而去,弗得與之言。

FORGET WHAT I JUST SAID AND HEAD FOR THE CAPITAL.

BUT MASTER, AREN'T YOU GOING BACK ON YOUR WORD?

THE GODS DON'T RECOGNIZE PROMISES MADE UNDER DURESS.

WHEN DUKE LING OF WEI HEARD THAT CONFUCIUS WAS APPROACHING, HE WENT OUTSIDE THE CITY GATES TO WELCOME HIM.

UNFORTUNATELY, I'M GETTING OLD AND SO HAVE NO USE FOR YOU...

IF SOMEONE WOULD LET ME HAVE CONTROL OF THE GOVERNMENT, I'D HAVE EVERYTHING IN ORDER IN A YEAR, AND WITHIN THREE YEARS, THE COUNTRY WOULD BE THRIVING AND PROSPEROUS.

SIGH.

於是孔子自楚反乎衛。是歲也，孔子年六十三，而魯哀公六年也。

其明年，吳與魯會繒，徵百牢。太宰嚭召季康子。康子使子貢往，然後得已。

孔子曰：「魯衛之政，兄弟也。」是時，衛君輒父不得立，在外，諸侯數以為讓。而孔子弟子多仕於衛，衛君欲得孔子為政。子路曰：「衛君待子而為政，子將奚先？」孔子曰：「必也正名乎！」子路曰：「有是哉，子之迂也！奚其正也？」孔子曰：「野哉由也！夫名不正則言不順，言不順則事不成，事不成則禮

57

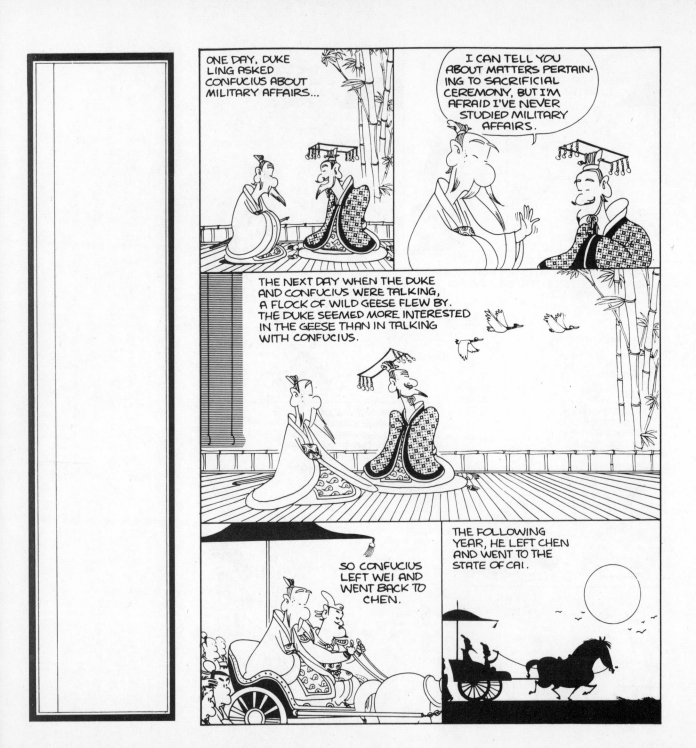

ONE DAY, DUKE LING ASKED CONFUCIUS ABOUT MILITARY AFFAIRS...

I CAN TELL YOU ABOUT MATTERS PERTAINING TO SACRIFICIAL CEREMONY, BUT I'M AFRAID I'VE NEVER STUDIED MILITARY AFFAIRS.

THE NEXT DAY WHEN THE DUKE AND CONFUCIUS WERE TALKING, A FLOCK OF WILD GEESE FLEW BY. THE DUKE SEEMED MORE INTERESTED IN THE GEESE THAN IN TALKING WITH CONFUCIUS.

SO CONFUCIUS LEFT WEI AND WENT BACK TO CHEN.

THE FOLLOWING YEAR, HE LEFT CHEN AND WENT TO THE STATE OF CAI.

ANOTHER YEAR PASSED, AND CONFUCIUS LEFT CAI FOR THE TINY FIEFDOM OF SHE, WHERE HE GAINED AN AUDIENCE WITH THE DUKE.

WHAT ARE THE PRINCIPLES OF GOVERNING?

THE PROPER WAY OF GOVERNING IS TO WIN THE ALLEGIANCE OF PEOPLE FAR AWAY AND TO GAIN THE ADHERENCE OF THOSE NEARBY.

ZHONG YOU, WHAT'S YOUR MASTER LIKE?

I'M AFRAID I DON'T KNOW HOW TO DESCRIBE HIM,...

THE DUKE ASKED ME TO DESCRIBE YOU, AND I DIDN'T KNOW WHAT TO SAY...

ZHONG YOU, WHY DIDN'T YOU SAY, "HE'S A MAN WHO NEVER TIRES OF STUDYING THE WAY AND NEVER GETS BORED WITH TEACHING,

"WHEN HE STUDIES, HE IS SO DILIGENT THAT HE FORGETS TO EAT, AND WHEN HAPPY, ALL OF HIS TROUBLES ARE FORGOTTEN,

"TO THE POINT THAT HE DOESN'T EVEN REALIZE OLD AGE IS CREEPING UP ON HIM."

固之，則可矣。」而衞孔文子將攻太叔，問策於仲尼。仲尼辭不知，退而命載而行，曰：「鳥能擇木，木豈能擇鳥乎！」文子固止。會季康子逐公華、公賓、公林，以幣迎孔子，孔子歸魯。

孔子之去魯凡十四歲而反乎魯。

魯哀公問政，對曰：「政在選臣。季康子問政，曰：「舉直錯諸枉，則枉者直。」康子患盜，孔子曰：「苟子之不欲，雖賞之不竊。」然魯終不能用孔子，孔子亦不求仕。

59

CONFUCIUS LEFT SHE AND RETURNED TO CAI. HERE, HE AGAIN ENCOUNTERED WU INVADING CHEN, AND CHU COMING TO THE AID OF CHEN;

AND IN THE MIDST OF ALL THE DEVASTATION AND CONFUSION, CONFUCIUS FOUND HIMSELF CAUGHT BETWEEN CAI AND CHEN WITHOUT ACCESS TO ANY FOOD.

HIS STUDENTS BEGAN TO FEEL THE ADVERSE EFFECTS OF PROLONGED HUNGER, BUT CONFUCIUS CONTINUED TO TEACH AND RECITE, TO PLAY THE ZITHER AND SING.

GROWL

IS THIS WHAT BEING A GENTLEMAN COMES TO?

CLANG!

THERE WILL BE TIMES LIKE THIS. BUT IN TIMES OF DISTRESS, A GENTLEMAN PERSEVERES AND MAINTAINS HIS DIGNITY, WHILE A LESSER MAN LOSES CONTROL AND COMMITS UNSEEMLY ACTS.

孔子之時，周室微而禮樂廢，詩書缺。追迹三代之禮，序書傳，上紀唐虞之際，下至秦繆，編次其事。

曰：「夏禮吾能言之，杞不足徵也。殷禮吾能言之，宋不足徵也。足，則吾能徵之矣。」觀殷夏所損益

曰：「後雖百世可知也，以一文一質。周監二代，郁郁乎文哉。吾從周。」故書傳、禮記自孔氏。

孔子語魯大師：「樂其可知也。始作翕如，縱之純如，皦如，繹如也，以成。」「吾自衛反魯，然後

樂正，雅頌各得其所。」

IN THE ELEVENTH YEAR OF LU DUKE AI, WHEN CONFUCIUS WAS SIXTY-EIGHT YEARS OLD, JISUN FEI WELCOMED CONFUCIUS BACK TO LU WITH A LARGE EMOLUMENT.

CONFUCIUS HAD BEEN AWAY FROM LU TRAVELING THE LAND FOR FOURTEEN YEARS BEFORE RETURNING.

DUKE AI AND JISUN OFTED ASKED CONFUCIUS ABOUT PRINCIPLES OF GOVERNING, BUT THEY NEVER PUT HIS SUGGESTIONS TO USE.

CONFUCIUS NO LONGER ENTERTAINED VISIONS OF BECOMING A GOVERNMENT OFFICIAL, INSTEAD UTILIZING HIS POSITION AS SCHOLAR-LAUREATE TO COMPILE THE *BOOK OF SONGS* AND THE *BOOK OF HISTORY*, TO EDIT THE *BOOK OF CEREMONY* AND THE *BOOK OF MUSIC*, TO COMMENT ON THE *BOOK OF CHANGES*, AND TO WRITE THE *SPRING & AUTUMN ANNALS*...

SONGS & HISTORY

BOOK OF CHANGES

CEREMONY & MUSIC

SPRING & AUTUMN ANNALS

古者詩三千餘篇，及至孔子，去其重，取可施於禮義，上采契后稷，中述殷周之盛，至幽厲之缺，始於衽席，故曰「關雎之亂以為風始，鹿鳴為小雅始，文王為大雅始，清廟為頌始」。三百五篇孔子皆弦歌之，以求合韶武雅頌之音。禮樂自此可得而述，以備王道，成六藝。

孔子晚而喜易，序彖、繫、象、說卦、文言。讀易，韋編三絕。曰：「假我數年，若是，我於易則彬彬矣。」

61

言，侃侃如也。

其於鄉黨，恂恂似不能言者。其於宗廟朝廷，辯辯言，唯謹爾。朝，與上大夫言，誾誾如也；與下大夫

仁。不憤不啓，舉一隅不以三隅反，則弗復也。

孔子以四教：文，行，忠，信。絶四：毋意，毋必，毋固，毋我。所愼：齊，戰，疾。子罕言利與命與

孔子以詩書禮樂教，弟子蓋三千焉，身通六藝者七十有二人。如顏濁鄒之徒，頗受業者甚衆。

HE LECTURED AND TAUGHT HIS DISCIPLES BETWEEN THE BANKS OF THE ZHU AND SI RIVERS...

CONFUCIUS DID NOT DISCRIMINATE BETWEEN RICH AND POOR, HIGH STATION OR LOW. HE ACCEPTED ALL STUDENTS THAT CAME TO HIM, TEACHING EACH ACCORDING TO THE STUDENT'S ABILITY.

CONFUCIUS INITIATED THE FOUR TEACHINGS:
*CULTURE
CONDUCT
CONSCIENTIOUSNESS
TRUSTWORTHINESS*

HE ALSO ESTABLISHED THE EIGHT STEPS IN LEARNING, SELF-CULTIVATION, AND CONDUCT:

3 Aims: Illustrious Virtue
• Loving the People
• Resting in the Highest Good

*INVESTIGATION OF THINGS
EXTENSION OF KNOWLEDGE
SINCERITY OF THOUGHT
RECTIFICATION OF THE MIND
CULTIVATION OF THE PERSON
REGULATION OF THE FAMILY
ORDER IN THE STATE
PEACE THROUGHOUT THE LAND*

62

FURTHERMORE, THE STUDENTS WERE EXPECTED TO ATTAIN THE THREE VIRTUES OF WISDOM, BENEVOLENCE, AND COURAGE THROUGH THEIR MASTERY OF THE SIX ARTS: CEREMONY, MUSIC, ARCHERY, CHARIOTEERING, CALLIGRAPHY, AND MATHEMATICS.

CONFUCIUS' TEACHINGS CAN BE DISTINGUISHED INTO FOUR AREAS OF EMPHASIS:

RESOLVING YOURSELF ON THE WAY

RESIDING IN VIRTUE

RELYING ON BENEVOLENCE

REVELING IN THE ARTS

LITERATURE

GOVERNING

SPEECH

VIRTUE

TAKE VIRTUOUS CONDUCT AS PRIMARY, SPEECH AS SECONDARY TO IT, GOVERNING AS SECONDARY TO THAT, AND LITERATURE AS THE LAST.

入公門，鞠躬如也；趨進，翼如也。君召使儐，色勃如也。君命召，不俟駕行矣。

魚餒，肉敗，割不正，不食。席不正，不坐。食於有喪者之側，未嘗飽也。

是日哭，則不歌。見齊衰、瞽者，雖童子必變。

「三人行，必得我師。」「德之不脩，學之不講，聞義不能徙，不善不能改，是吾憂也。」使人歌，

善，則使復之，然后和之。 子不語：怪、力、亂、神。

63

IN THE SIXTEENTH YEAR OF LU DUKE AI, CONFUCIUS FELL ILL...

MASTER...

ZIGONG! WHAT TOOK YOU SO LONG?

IS THIS HOW TAI MOUNTAIN SHALL COME TUMBLING DOWN?

IS THIS HOW BEAMS AND COLUMNS CRUMBLE? IS THIS HOW PHILOSOPHERS WITHER AWAY?

THE WORLD HAS LOST THE WAY FOR A LONG TIME NOW, AND NOBODY IS ABLE TO FOLLOW MY IDEALS OF GOVERNING.

子貢曰：「夫子之文章，可得聞也。夫子言天道與性命，弗可得聞也已。」顏淵喟然歎曰：「仰之彌高，鑽之彌堅。瞻之在前，忽焉在後。夫子循循然善誘人，博我以文，約我以禮，欲罷不能。既竭我才，如有所立，卓爾。雖欲從之，蔑由也已。」達巷黨人曰：「大哉孔子，博學而無所成名。」子聞之曰：「我何執？執御乎？執射乎？我執御矣。」牢曰：「子云：『不試，故藝』。」

魯哀公十四年春，狩大野。叔孫氏車子鉏商獲獸，以為不祥。仲尼視之，曰：「麟也。」取之。曰：

64

SEVEN DAYS LATER, CONFUCIUS PASSED AWAY.

HE DIED ON THE TWENTY-SIXTH DAY OF THE FOURTH MONTH, IN THE SIXTEENTH YEAR OF DUKE AI, AT THE AGE OF SEVENTY-THREE...

THE GRAND HISTORIAN SIMA QIAN SAYS, "IT IS WRITTEN IN THE *BOOK OF SONGS* THUS: 'WE EMULATE VIRTUOUS CONDUCT AS WE LOOK UP TO LOFTY MOUNTAINS.'

"CONFUCIUS WAS A COMMONER WHOSE TEACHINGS HAVE BEEN TRANSMITTED FOR MORE THAN TEN GENERATIONS, AND THERE IS NO INTELLECTUAL WHO DOES NOT CONSIDER HIM HIS TEACHER. CONFUCIUS WAS INDEED THE GREATEST OF ALL SAGES!"

CONFUCIUS R.I.P.

「河不出圖，雛不出書，吾已矣夫！」顏淵死，孔子曰：「天喪予！」及西狩見麟，曰：「吾道窮矣！」喟然歎曰：「莫知我夫！」子貢曰：「何為莫知子？」子曰：「不怨天，不尤人，下學而上達，知我者其天乎！」

「不降其志，不辱其身，伯夷、叔齊乎！」謂「柳下惠、少連降志辱身矣」。謂「虞仲、夷逸隱居放言，行中清，廢中權」。「我則異於是，無可無不可。」

65

# The Analects

THE ANALECTS

「論語」是誰寫的？誰編的？東漢班固在漢書藝文志六藝略，有所說明：

論語者，孔子應答弟子、時人，及弟子相與言，而接聞於夫子之語也。當時弟子各有所記，夫子既卒，門人相與輯而論纂，故謂之論語。

由此認為：「論語」是孔子和他的門人或時人的談話，以及門人彼此的談話記錄。

67

PLEASURE AND HUMILITY

IS IT NOT PLEASURABLE TO STUDY AND PRACTICE WHAT ONE LEARNS?

IS IT NOT DELIGHTFUL TO HAVE FRIENDS COME FROM AFAR?

IS HE NOT A GENTLEMAN WHO REMAINS DIGNIFIED THOUGH GOING UNRECOGNIZED?

首章第一句為「子曰：學而時習之，」故取「學而」二字，作為本篇篇名。以下各篇同。

古人著書，往往取第一句中第一二字做標題，別無他義，如詩經、論語、孟子都是如此。本篇

●這裏的「亦」，乃是一個加重語氣的助詞。

●之，指所學得的知識言。

●習，通常有溫習、實習兩種意思。

●學，是指學修己的道理和學濟世利人的知識。

●論語中的子字，是孔子弟子對孔子專用的尊稱。

# SELF-CRITIQUE

CONFUCIUS' PUPIL ZENGZI SAID:

EVERY DAY I CRITIQUE MYSELF IN THREE WAYS:

IN HELPING OTHERS, DID I NOT DO SO CONSCIENTIOUSLY?

IN INTERCOURSE WITH MY FRIENDS, WAS I NOT TRUSTWORTHY?

DID I NOT PRACTICE WHAT HAD BEEN TAUGHT ME BEFORE?

◉仲尼弟子列傳：「曾參，南武城人，字子輿；少孔子四十六歲。」

◉省，思察己之所行也。

◉為，于偽切，含有幫助意義。謀，是計議、計畫的意思；忠，是盡心力的意思。

◉傳，直專切。

【今譯】曾子說：「我每天以三件事情來反省我自己：我替人謀事，有沒有盡了心？我對朋友有沒有不誠信的地方？老師傳授我的，我溫習過了嗎？」

69

LIKE THE NORTH STAR

IF IN GOVERNING THE PEOPLE, YOU USE VIRTUE TO TRANSFORM THEM,

THEY WILL ALL PAY ALLEGIANCE TO YOU,

LIKE THE NORTH STAR, WHICH RESTS QUIETLY IN ITS PLACE WHILE ALL THE OTHER STARS REVOLVE AROUND IT.

● 「北辰」是北極星，中國古代天文學認為宇宙天體的中心是太極，在銀河北端，史記天官書：「中宮北極星，其一明者，太一（即北極）常居也。」北辰斗七星是陰陽動力的根源，觀測斗柄的旋轉以定歲時。

● 「共」同拱，是圍繞歸向的意思。

● 這是孔子說施政要行德化，人拱辰，可以無為而治。

【今譯】孔子說：「以仁德來施政，好像北極星一樣，高居在星座上，眾多星辰都圍繞歸向它。」

**CULTIVATING THE WAY**

WHEN I WAS FIFTEEN, I SET MY MIND ON LEARNING.

WHEN I WAS THIRTY, I COULD HOLD FIRM IN MY LEARNING WITHOUT THE LEAST BIT OF WAVERING.

propriety, balance

AT FORTY, THERE WAS NOTHING I DIDN'T KNOW ABOUT CONDUCTING AFFAIRS OR UNDERSTANDING PRINCIPLES.
wise

AT FIFTY, I UNDERSTOOD THE MANDATES OF HEAVEN, AND BECAUSE OF THIS, I BORE NO GRUDGE AGAINST HEAVEN NOR DID I BLAME OTHERS.

AT SIXTY, I COULD JUDGE A PERSON'S HONESTY AND CHARACTER SIMPLY BY HEARING THEM SPEAK
obedience to Mandates of Heaven
interconnectedness

AT SEVENTY, I BECAME ABLE TO SPEAK AND ACT SPONTANEOUSLY WITHOUT EVER TRANSGRESSING.
Freedom of Behavior
highest desire of human life

●説文：「吾，我自稱也。」

●有，讀音和意義都同「又」。乎，義同于或於

●立，是指能夠運用所學得的道理以立身行己。

●不惑，是不受異端、邪説所惑亂。

●劉疏：「天命者：説文云，『命，使也。』」言

天使己如此也。知天命者：知己為天所命，非虛生也。」

●這章乃是孔子自述生平修養的成就；所謂十五、三十等數目，只是舉一大概；讀者對於這些數目可不必太拘泥。

71

# TRUE UNDERSTANDING

**ZHONG YOU, DO YOU UNDERSTAND ALL THAT I'VE TAUGHT YOU?**

**IF YOU UNDERSTAND, SAY THAT YOU UNDERSTAND.**

**IF YOU DON'T UNDERSTAND, SAY THAT YOU DON'T UNDERSTAND.**

**ONLY BY SPEAKING TRUTHFULLY IS IT TRUE UNDERSTANDING!**

●這是孔子教誨子路不要自稱聰明，知是真理之事，不可模糊，要求進步，必先不自欺。

【今譯】孔子說：「仲由，我教你的，你都能知道麼？你知道的，你才說『知道』；你不知道的，你就要承認『不知道』：這就是真的『知道』啊！」

# PROPER CEREMONY

ONE DAY WHEN CONFUCIUS WENT TO THE DUKE OF ZHOU TEMPLE TO ASSIST IN THE SACRIFICE, HE INQUIRED ABOUT EVERY ASPECT OF THE CEREMONY.

WHO SAID THIS GUY FROM ZOU KNOWS ANYTHING ABOUT CEREMONY? HE COMES TO A SACRIFICE HERE AND ASKS ABOUT EVERY LITTLE THING.

ASKING QUESTIONS, BEING HUMBLE RATHER THAN PRESUMING TO KNOW EVERYTHING-- THIS IS PROPER CEREMONY!

●大音泰；漢石經作太。包曰，「大廟，周公廟。」

●「每事問」，是指問每件不確切知道的事情。

●鄹，地名；是孔子的家鄉。說文和左傳字作陬。這裏的「鄹人」，指孔子的父親陬人紇，史記作叔梁紇。

【今譯】孔子進入太廟，對每一件有關太廟祭典的事都要向人請教。有人說：「誰説鄹人的兒子懂得禮？他進入太廟，每件事都要問！」孔子聽了這話，説：「這就是禮呀！」

73

## THE SACRIFICIAL GOAT

CONFUCIUS' DISCIPLE ZIGONG WANTED TO ELIMINATE THE GOAT FROM AN ANCIENT SACRIFICIAL CEREMONY THAT HAD LOST ITS PARTICULAR SIGNIFICANCE.

MASTER, CAN WE DO WITHOUT THE GOAT?

ZIGONG, WHAT YOU CARE ABOUT IS THE GOAT.

WHAT I CARE ABOUT IS THE CEREMONY.

●朔，是中國舊曆每月的第一天。告朔，是天子把一年十二月的朔政（曆書）布告給諸侯。告朔之餼羊，是每個諸侯的國家所預備的生羊用以招待天子頒曆的使臣的。在孔子的時侯，天子既沒有頒曆的事情，而魯國每年所預備的餼羊也只是空設，所以子貢想要廢止這個餼羊的供給。

●愛，是「捨不得」的意思。

【今譯】子貢想要把告朔的餼羊廢止了。孔子説：「賜，你捨不得那隻羊；我卻捨不得那個禮啊！」

THE WAY OF SELF-RESPECT

IF A TRUE STUDENT SETS HIS MIND ON STUDYING THE WAY,

AND YET IS ASHAMED OF THE CLOTHES HE WEARS,

OR THE FOOD HE EATS,

HE IS NOT WORTH DISCUSSING THE WAY WITH !

【今譯】孔子說：「一個有志於天下太平的人，如果還以自身的衣食不美好而認為是可恥，那便不足道了！」

● 這裡的「道」字，可解釋為「天下有道」。

● 「未足以議」，意為「不足與之論道」。

75

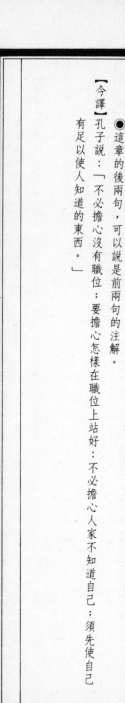

【今譯】孔子說：「不必擔心沒有職位；要擔心怎樣在職位上站好：不必擔心人家不知道自己；須先使自己有足以使人知道的東西。」

●這章的後兩句，可以說是前兩句的注解。

WHAT IT TAKES

DON'T WORRY ABOUT NOT HAVING A POSITION,

WORRY INSTEAD ABOUT WHETHER OR NOT YOU HAVE WHAT IT TAKES TO HOLD A POSITION.

DON'T WORRY ABOUT OTHER PEOPLE NOT KNOWING ABOUT YOU,

PURSUE INSTEAD QUALITIES THAT ARE WORTH KNOWING ABOUT.

SEEING YOURSELF IN OTHERS

WHEN YOU SEE SOMEONE WHO IS CAPABLE AND VIRTUOUS, THINK ABOUT TRYING TO BE LIKE HIM.

WHEN YOU SEE SOMEONE WHO IS NEITHER CAPABLE NOR VIRTUOUS,

LOOK AT YOURSELF,

AND SEE IF YOU SHARE ANY QUALITIES WITH HIM.

【今譯】孔子說：「見到賢人，便用心學他，與他看齊；見到不賢的人，便反省自己有沒有和他一樣的缺點

●包曰：「思與賢者等。」

●省，鄭注：「省，察也；察己得無然也。」

77

【今譯】孔子說，「父母在的時候，不到遠處去遊；如出遊，必有一定的地方。」

●鄭曰：「方，猶常也。」但晉語七：「祈奚曰：午之少也，遊有鄉。」以常釋方，不如以鄉釋方。所以此處「方」，亦可解為「地方」。

●此孔子教人體念親心，不使多所憂慮。

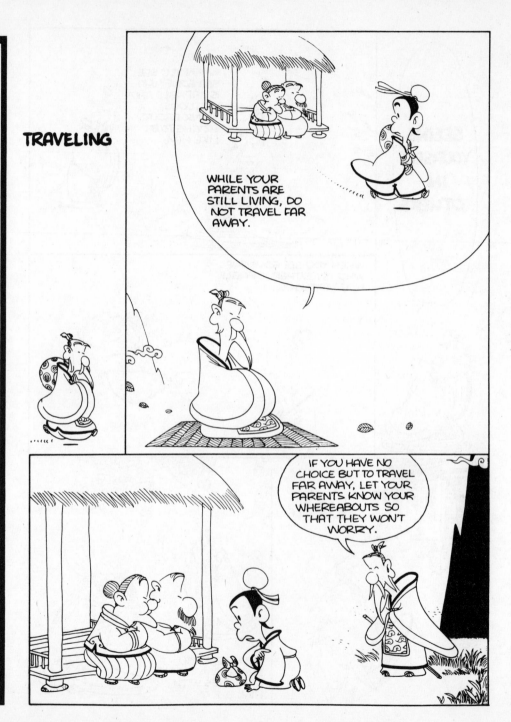

TRAVELING

WHILE YOUR PARENTS ARE STILL LIVING, DO NOT TRAVEL FAR AWAY.

IF YOU HAVE NO CHOICE BUT TO TRAVEL FAR AWAY, LET YOUR PARENTS KNOW YOUR WHEREABOUTS SO THAT THEY WON'T WORRY.

78

FRIENDS OF VIRTUE

A MAN WHO HAS VIRTUE WILL NEVER BE LONELY;

OTHERS LIKE HIMSELF WILL ALWAYS BE NEAR.

●周禮遂人：五家為鄰。韓詩外傳：八家為鄰。今人毛子水先生以為，居相近為鄰，故引申有親近義。

【今譯】孔子說：「有道德的人決不會孤立，必有同類相從，就知道住處必有鄰居一樣。」

## YAN HUI'S INTELLECT

ONE DAY, CONFUCIUS SAID TO ZIGONG:

WHO IS BETTER, YOU OR YAN HUI?

HOW CAN I BE COMPARED WITH YAN HUI?

IF YOU TELL YAN HUI ONE THING, HE CAN EXTRAPOLATE TEN MORE THINGS FROM THAT.

IF YOU TELL ME SOMETHING, I CAN ONLY FIGURE OUT TWO MORE THINGS.

YOU'RE RIGHT, YOU'RE NOT AS GOOD AS HE IS. NEITHER YOU NOR I ARE AS GOOD AS HE IS.

【今譯】孔子對子貢説：「你和顏回，那個好一點？」子貢回答説：「我怎麼敢跟顏回比！顏回聞一知十；我只可聞一知二。」孔子説：「你不及他麼？我和你都不及他啊！」

● 女音汝。

●「弗如也」的「也」字，可作疑問詞解。

● 包曰：「既然子貢不如，復云吾與女俱不如者，蓋欲以慰子貢也。」

80

# YOU CAN'T CARVE ROTTEN WOOD

ONCE WHEN CONFUCIUS' DISCIPLE ZAI YU WAS SLEEPING IN THE MIDDLE OF THE DAY...

YOU CAN'T CARVE ROTTEN WOOD, AND YOU CAN'T WHITEWASH A FILTHY WALL.

BUT WHAT'S THE USE ADMONISHING A PERSON LIKE ZAI YU!

I USED TO LISTEN TO WHAT PEOPLE SAID AND THEN ASSUME THAT THEY WOULD DO JUST WHAT THEY SAID THEY WOULD.

BUT NOW AFTER LISTENING TO SOMEONE, I WAIT AND SEE IF WHAT THEY DO IS THE SAME AS WHAT THEY SAID. ZAI YU HELPED CHANGE MY THINKING ON THIS.

●糞土，是掃除土地所得的穢土。

●說文：杇，所以涂也；涂同塗字。杇，本是用以粉飾也叫杇。

●「與」在此處為語助詞。經傳釋詞四：「與，猶『也』也。」

●行，下孟切。

●「於予與改是」是說：我之所以會有這種改變，是從宰予引起的。

●「誅」是責備的意思。

81

# THE MEANING OF "CULTURED"

子貢問孔子說：孔文子為什麼稱為文呢？孔文子名圉，是衞國大夫。他要大叔疾和妻離婚，疾不聽，文子怒，要帶兵去抓他，而先去請問孔子。孔子認為這樣做是不對的，不給他回答。孔文子為人如此，子貢懷疑為什麼他死後還稱為文呢？孔子說：他聰明而能好學，不以下問為恥，這是可以稱為文了。因為一般的人，聰明的多不好學，地位高的多不肯下問，所以孔子不隱沒孔文子的善處。

ZIGONG ASKED CONFUCIUS:

HOW DID KONG WENZI GET THE NAME WEN "CULTURED"?

HE WAS NATURALLY INTELLIGENT AND ENJOYED LEARNING,

AND HE WAS NOT ASHAMED OF LEARNING EVEN FROM HIS INFERIORS.

THIS IS WHY HE IS CALLED WEN.

## CONTRIVING APPEARANCES

TO SPEAK FLATTERING WORDS, TO CONTRIVE AN INGRATIATING APPEARANCE, AND TO BE OVERLY RESPECTFUL...

THE SCHOLAR ZUOQIU MING FOUND THIS KIND OF BEHAVIOR SHAMEFUL. I, TOO, FIND IT SHAMEFUL.

TO INSINCERELY BEFRIEND A PERSON YOU REALLY DETEST...

ZUOQIU MING FOUND THIS KIND OF BEHAVIOR SHAMEFUL. I, TOO, FIND IT SHAMEFUL.

●皇疏引繆協曰，「足恭者，以恭足於人意而不合於禮度。」集注：「足，過也。」

【今譯】孔子說：「一個人話說得好聽，臉色裝得好看，態度做得太過恭敬：這回樣子，左丘明認為是可恥的；我也認為是可恥。心裏怨恨一個人，表面卻和他友善，這種事情，左丘明以為可恥；我也以為可恥。」

83

WISHES

ONE DAY WHEN YAN HUI AND ZHONG YOU WERE ACCOMPANYING CONFUCIUS...

WHY DON'T EACH OF YOU TELL ME WHAT YOU HAVE YOUR MINDS SET ON.

I WISH TO BE ABLE TO LEND MY HORSES AND CARRIAGE, CLOTHES AND FURS TO OTHERS, AND IF THEY GET RUINED, TO NOT REGRET HAVING LENT THEM.

I WISH TO NOT BOAST ABOUT MY STRENGTHS

AND TO NOT SHIRK MY TROUBLES OFF ON OTHERS.

WE ALSO WISH TO HEAR WHAT THE MASTER HAS HIS MIND SET ON.

FOR OLD PEOPLE TO BE WELL CARED FOR,

FRIENDS TO BE TRUSTWORTHY,

AND CHILDREN TO BE CHERISHED.

●鄭注：「盍，何不也。」裘，皮衣。敝，意同「壞」；「之」，是指車馬衣裘；憾，意同恨。

●伐，是自誇的意思。無伐善，是不誇說自己的好處。無施勞，意指不把煩難的事推到別人身上。

●「老者、安之」等三句的「之」字，分別指「老者、朋友、少者」。

84

A TOWN OF TEN FAMILIES

IN A SMALL TOWN OF ONLY TEN FAMILIES,

THERE IS SURE TO BE SOMEONE WHOSE CONSCIENTIOUSNESS AND TRUSTWORTHINESS MATCH MINE,

THERE JUST WON'T BE ANYONE WHO LIKES TO LEARN AS MUCH AS I DO.

◉ 十室之邑，是指很小的一個地方。

◉ 劉疏：「忠信者，質之至美者也。然有美質必濟之以學，斯可祛其所蔽而進於知仁之道。」

◉ 好，呼報切。「好學」，指不懈於求知而能以學修德言。

【今譯】孔子説，「就是一個很小的地方，也一定會有像我一樣忠信的人；如果他有不及我的地方，那是因為他不像我這麼好學。」

85

## YAN HUI'S LEARNING

**ONE DAY, DUKE AI OF LU ASKED CONFUCIUS:**

**WHICH ONE OF YOUR STUDENTS LIKES TO LEARN THE MOST?**

**THERE WAS ONE CALLED YAN HUI WHO MOST ENJOYED LEARNING.**

**IF HE EVER LOST HIS TEMPER, HE REALIZED IT AND STEADIED HIMSELF IMMEDIATELY.**

**AND HE NEVER MADE THE SAME MISTAKE TWICE.**

**UNFORTUNATELY, HE DIED YOUNG. AND I HAVE YET TO FIND ONE WHO ENJOYS LEARNING AS MUCH AS HIM.**

●遷有遷延的意思；貳有重複的意思。

●易繫辭下：「子曰，顏氏之子，其殆庶幾乎！有不善，未嘗不知；知之，未嘗復行也。」

●集注：「遷，移也。怒於甲者不移於乙。」毛子水先生認為，集注說亦可通，但解「不遷」為「發而便止」更可證明「好學」。

【今譯】哀公問孔子：「你的弟子中誰最好學？」孔子說道：「有個叫顏回的最好學：他若發怒，便會立刻化解；他犯了過，決不會再犯。可惜短命死了！現在就沒有聽見這樣好學的人。」

86

YAN HUI'S WORTHINESS

YAN HUI WAS CERTAINLY CAPABLE AND VIRTUOUS!

A SMALL BOWL OF RICE,

A LADLEFUL OF WATER,

AND A RUN-DOWN COTTAGE.

OTHER PEOPLE CAN'T TAKE SUCH POVERTY, BUT IT NEVER AFFECTED YAN HUI'S CHEERFULNESS.

YAN HUI WAS CERTAINLY CAPABLE AND VIRTUOUS!

●賈子道術：「行道者謂之賢。」

●簞，竹器，可用來盛飯。食音嗣，義同飯。

●瓢，義同瓢，可用以盛水。

●樂音洛。

【今譯】孔子說：「顏回真賢！一碗飯，一杯水，住在狹窄的巷子裏：這種生活，要是別人，一定要憂愁得難以忍受了；顏回還是自得其樂。顏回真賢！」

87

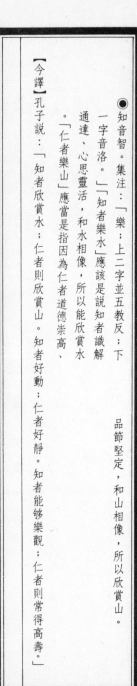

【今譯】孔子説：「知者欣賞水；仁者則欣賞山。知者好動；仁者好静。知者能夠樂觀；仁者則常得高壽。」

●知音智。集注：「樂：上二字並五教反；下一字音洛。」「知者樂水」應該是説知者識解通達、心思靈活，和水相像，所以能欣賞水。「仁者樂山」應當是指因為仁者道德崇高、品節堅定，和山相像，所以欣賞山。

THE WISE AND THE BENEVOLENT

WISE PEOPLE ENJOY THE WATER. THEY UNDERSTAND THE HAPPENINGS OF THE WORLD AND SO TAKE PLEASURE IN THE SMOOTH FLOWING OF THE WATER.

BENEVOLENT PEOPLE ENJOY THE MOUNTAINS. THEY ARE STEADFAST IN THEIR VIRTUE AND SO TAKE PLEASURE IN THE UNWAVERING OF THE MOUNTAINS.

WISE PEOPLE ENJOY BEING ACTIVE.

BENEVOLENT PEOPLE ENJOY KEEPING STILL.

WISE PEOPLE FIND THEIR OWN JOYS.

BENEVOLENT PEOPLE LIVE LONG IN TRANQUILITY.

88

TRANSMITTING IDEAS

I TRANSMIT IDEAS RATHER THAN CREATE THEM.

I BELIEVE IN THE PRINCIPLES OF THE TANG, YU, XIA, SHANG, AND ZHOU DYNASTY FOUNDERS AND TAKE DELIGHT IN ANCIENT CULTURE.

AND I PRIVATELY EMULATE OLD PENG, THE CAPABLE AND VIRTUOUS MINISTER OF THE SHANG DYNASTY.

●漢書儒林傳：「周道既衰，陵夷二百餘年而孔子興；究觀古今之篇籍，因近聖之事以立先王之教。故曰，述而不作，信而好古。」

●廣雅釋詁四：「竊，私也。」廣雅疏證：「竊，謂私比也。」「竊」，含有謙意。

●鄭注：「老，老聃；彭，彭祖。」

【今譯】孔子說：「我循述古人的遺法而不自己創作；我信服古人，並且喜愛古人；在這些事情上，我敢私自比於老、彭。」

89

A SCHOLAR'S EASE

TO QUIETLY RECITE AND MEMORIZE THE CLASSICS,

TO LOVE LEARNING WITHOUT TIRING OF IT,

TO NEVER BE BORED WITH TEACHING,

HOW COULD THESE BE DIFFICULT FOR ME?

●識音志。集注：「識，記也。默識，謂不言而存諸心也。」

【今譯】孔子說：「把聽到的、見到的、牢記在心裏；孜孜的勤求學問而不厭；諄諄的教誨他人而不倦：這些事情，實在都是很平常的！」

●「何有於我哉」意思是：這些事我雖能做到，但都是不足稱道的。

90

DREAMING OF THE DUKE OF ZHOU

ZZZ

Z

OH, I'M GETTING SO OLD...

IT'S BEEN SO LONG SINCE I DREAMED OF THE DUKE OF ZHOU!

●孔子一直希望有個太平世界，所以常常想到周室太平的時候，因而常常夢見周公。現在孔子覺得，他所以好久沒有夢見周公，應當是由於年老力衰、志道不篤的緣故。因此發出這樣的感歎。不過，也可以看出，孔子到老年時，最關心的還是天下太平。

【今譯】孔子說，「我已衰老得太厲害；我已好久沒有夢見周公了！」

91

RESOLVE YOURSELF ON THE WAY.

DAO 道

## THE FOUNDATION OF GOOD CONDUCT

RELY ON VIRTUE.

RESIDE IN BENEVOLENCE.

REVEL IN THE ARTS.

●這裏的「道」，與「朝聞道」的「道」同義，是指「天下有道」，亦即「天下太平」。

●德是「為政以德」「道之以德」的「德」，和武力、詐謀是相反的。

●仁是孔子所認為最高的德行的。

●游是熟習的意思；「藝」，是處理事務的技能。

【今譯】孔子説：「一個人應該以天下太平為職志；求天下太平，只須用德行；德行則要以仁為主；據德依仁之外，還要熟習政事的處理。」

92

# UNIVERSAL EDUCATION

FOR ANYONE WHO BRINGS EVEN THE SMALLEST TOKEN OF APPRECIATION,

I HAVE YET TO REFUSE INSTRUCTION.

●脩，乾肉。古人以十脡為一束；束脩，是十脡乾肉。五條乾肉做一束，每條於中間受束處屈為兩脡；古人行相見禮的時候，束脩是很普通的禮物。

【今譯】孔子說：「有人來求學，祇要奉送拜師的禮物，不論他禮物的輕重，我總是一樣地教誨他。」

93

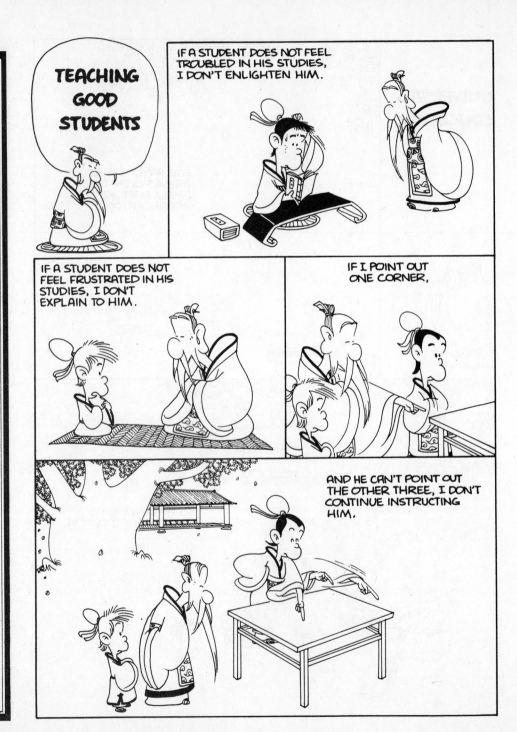

TEACHING GOOD STUDENTS

IF A STUDENT DOES NOT FEEL TROUBLED IN HIS STUDIES, I DON'T ENLIGHTEN HIM.

IF A STUDENT DOES NOT FEEL FRUSTRATED IN HIS STUDIES, I DON'T EXPLAIN TO HIM.

IF I POINT OUT ONE CORNER,

AND HE CAN'T POINT OUT THE OTHER THREE, I DON'T CONTINUE INSTRUCTING HIM.

● 學生自己不知道發憤求學，老師就不要啓示他；發憤是努力。啓是開導。悱是心裏想表達而未能。學生自己想表達而不能做到，老師不要去啓發他；隅是角，物有四角，舉一

可知其三。反是還以相證的意思。復是再告。老師指示事物的一方面給學生看，而學生不能自己推想其他方面，老師便可不必再告訴他。這都是説要學生自己去思考。

94

**SIMPLE PLEASURES**

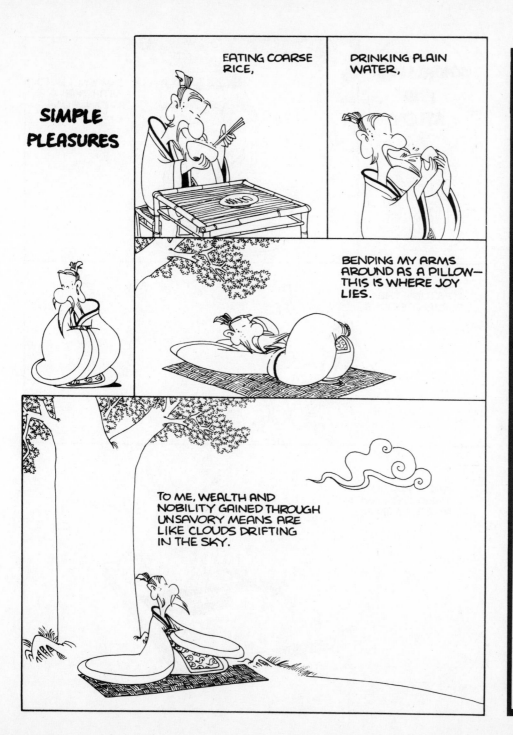

EATING COARSE RICE,

DRINKING PLAIN WATER,

BENDING MY ARMS AROUND AS A PILLOW— THIS IS WHERE JOY LIES.

TO ME, WEALTH AND NOBILITY GAINED THROUGH UNSAVORY MEANS ARE LIKE CLOUDS DRIFTING IN THE SKY.

◉ 飯，扶晚切，意為吃。疏，義同粗；食音嗣，意為飯食。疏食，粗米飯。

◉ 說文：「臂，手上也。肱，臂上也。」枕，之任切；「曲肱而枕之」，謂臥時用肱作枕。

【今譯】孔子說：「吃粗米飯，喝白水，彎起來當枕頭；這樣子的生活，亦自有其中樂趣。要是因不義而得到富貴，那富貴就像天上的浮雲，我是毫不關心的！」

95

KNOWLEDGE AND STUDY

I WASN'T BORN WITH THE KNOWLEDGE I HAVE;

I JUST LIKE TO STUDY THE ANCIENT BOOKS,

AND I PURSUE THEIR IDEAS WITH A KEEN MIND.

● 季氏篇：「孔子曰，生而知之者，上也；學而知之者，次也。」孔子認為知識是可求而得的。

【今譯】孔子說：「我並不是生下來就什麼都知道的；我只是喜好古代聖哲留下來的知識，並且勉力學來的。」

**LEARNING FROM OTHERS**

IF THERE ARE THREE PEOPLE WALKING ALONG, THERE WILL CERTAINLY BE ONE I CAN LEARN FROM.

I NOTICE THEIR STRONG POINTS AND WORK TO EMULATE THEM;

I ALSO NOTICE THEIR DEFECTS AND TRY TO CHANGE IF I FIND THEM IN MYSELF AS WELL.

HA HA HA

◉錢坫論語後錄：「子產曰，『其所善者吾則行之；其所惡者吾則改之』：是吾師也。」此云善、不善，當作是解；非謂三人中有善不善也。

◉子張篇：子貢曰，「夫子焉不學！而亦何常師之有！」

【今譯】三個人一起同行，其中必定有可以做我老師的，選擇他們的好處學習它，看出他們不好處，自己也可改正過來。

97

**FAIR PLAY**

CONFUCIUS WOULD USE A FISHING POLE TO CATCH FISH,

BUT HE WOULDN'T USE A NET.

HE'D SHOOT BIRDS,

BUT NOT WHILE THEY WERE NESTING.

●經義述聞：「網乃網之誤。」御覽八三四
引鄭注：「網，謂為大索橫流屬釣。」
●弋音翼，本義為木樁，因音同假為隹
：隹，繳射飛鳥也。說文

●繳，生絲縷。
●射，食亦切。宿，息六切；指宿在鳥巢的鳥
而言。

【今譯】孔子釣魚，但不用網罟去捕魚；孔子也繳射飛鳥，但不射宿在鳥巢裏的鳥。

98

## DYING MEN DON'T LIE

ONE DAY WHEN ZENGZI WAS ILL, MENG JINGZI PAID A VISIT TO HIM.

TWEET

THE SONG OF A BIRD ABOUT TO DIE IS MELANCHOLY;

THE WORDS OF A MAN ABOUT TO DIE ARE HONEST.

THERE ARE THREE THINGS THAT A GENTLEMAN SHOULD EMPHASIZE IN REGARD TO THE WAY;

BY KEEPING YOUR FACIAL EXPRESSIONS AND DEMEANOR IN ACCORD WITH PROPRIETY, YOU CAN DISTANCE YOURSELF FROM COARSENESS AND FRIVOLITY; BY MAINTAINING A SOBER COUNTENANCE, YOU CAN KEEP FROM BEING RECKLESS AND YOU CAN APPROACH SINCERITY; BY SPEAKING REASONABLY AND PROPERLY, YOU CAN DISTANCE YOURSELF FROM SHALLOW AND ABSURD PRATTLINGS.

AS FOR ALL OF THE VARIOUS ASPECTS OF CEREMONY, THERE ARE PEOPLE TO PERFORM THEM.

◉ 孟敬之，魯大夫仲孫捷；孟武伯的兒子。

◉ 鄭曰：「此『道』，謂禮也。」

◉ 遠、近都去聲。

◉ 鄙，鄙陋；倍，詩也。

◉ 「籩豆」，是古代盛食物的器皿；「籩豆之事」，是指一切禮制上有定例的事情講。

◉ 有司，指主管的官吏。

99

【今譯】孔子說：「孜孜求學，好像來不及的樣子，還怕自己遺失。」

● 學如不及，是說，未學時勤勉用功，好像趕來不及的樣子；……把學會了，只怕忘掉的樣，還怕學得不好，自己遺失。

GOOD STUDENTS FEAR FORGETTING

WHEN STUDYING, IT ALWAYS SEEMS LIKE THERE'S NOT ENOUGH TIME,

AND ONCE SOMETHING IS LEARNED, THERE'S ALWAYS THE FEAR OF LOSING IT.

100

THE STREAM OF TIME

ALL THINGS THAT PASS ARE JUST LIKE THIS!

NIGHT AND DAY, IT NEVER STOPS.

◉ 夫音符。

◉ 孔子把歲月的遷流比作流水。奔流的水，也容易使人想到君子進德修業、自強不息的道理。

【今譯】孔子在河流旁說：「人世一切的消逝也就是（像流水）這樣的吧！日夜不曾或停！」

◉ 舍同捨，這是孔子慨歎歲月不留，光陰如逝水，而勉人努力求學。

101

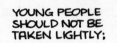

# AGE AND RESPECT

YOUNG PEOPLE SHOULD NOT BE TAKEN LIGHTLY;

WHO'S TO SAY THAT SOMEDAY THEY WON'T SURPASS OUR OWN GENERATION?

HOWEVER, IF A PERSON HAS REACHED FORTY OR FIFTY YEARS OLD AND IS STILL WITHOUT ACCOMPLISHMENT,

THAT PERSON IS NOT WORTH ONE'S RESPECT!

【今譯】孔子說：「青年後生的發展潛能未可限量是大可敬畏的，怎知道他將來的成就，不如現在的我呢？

祇是如果到了四十、五十歲還是無所成就，不為人知，那也就沒有什麼可畏的了。」

● 本章應是為警戒壯年人而發的。

● 這是勉勵青年要趁少壯時期努力上進，才不致蹉跎歲月。

102

**FACING FACTS**

A WISE PERSON WILL NEVER FEEL PERPLEXED.

A BENEVOLENT PERSON WILL NEVER WORRY.

AND A BRAVE PERSON FEARS NOTHING.

【今譯】孔子說：「有智慧的人不為事物所迷惑，有仁心的人不為困難而憂慮，有勇氣的人不為艱危而懼怯。」

● 知音智。

● 這三句也出現於憲問篇。

103

【今譯】馬房失火了。孔子剛從朝中回來，連忙問：「傷了人麼？」卻沒有問馬。

◉廄，馬房。

◉鄭玄以為「退朝」為「自魯君之朝來歸」。但鹽鐵論刑德篇卻認為：「魯廄焚；孔子罷朝，問人不問馬賤畜而重人也。」

FIRE IN THE STABLE
wise & benevolent

ONE DAY, CONFUCIUS' STABLE CAUGHT FIRE.

CONFUCIUS HURRIED HOME FROM THE COURT, AND THE FIRST WORDS OUT OF HIS MOUTH WERE:

IS ANYONE HURT?

HE DIDN'T ASK ABOUT THE HORSES.

SPIRITS AND DEATH

ZHONG YOU ASKED CONFUCIUS ABOUT SERVING SPIRITS AND GODS.

IF ONE DOESN'T YET UNDERSTAND HOW TO SERVE PEOPLE, HOW CAN ONE UNDERSTAND SERVING SPIRITS AND GODS?

MAY I INQUIRE ABOUT DEATH, THEN?

IF ONE DOESN'T YET UNDERSTAND LIFE, HOW CAN ONE UNDERSTAND DEATH?

●「事鬼神」，自是指祭祀的事情。但季路的意思，可能尚未脫去時俗所流行的迷信。

●「未能事人、焉能事鬼」，和答樊遲「務民之義，敬鬼神而遠之」的話同意。

【今譯】季路問怎樣服事鬼神。孔子說：「我們服事人都還服事不好，怎麼能夠服事鬼神呢！」季路接著又問人死後是怎樣的。孔子說：「我們對人活著時的道理都還沒有知道清楚，怎麼能夠知道死後的情形呢！」

105

OVERDOING IT

WHICH ONE IS MORE CAPABLE AND VIRTUOUS, ZIZHANG OR ZIXIA?

ZIZHANG OVERDOES IT...

AND ZIXIA FALLS SHORT.

THEN ZIZHANG IS THE BETTER ONE?

OVERDOING IT IS STILL FALLING SHORT!

●集注：「子張才高意廣，而好為苟難，故常過中；子夏篤信謹守、而規模狹隘，故常不及。」

●集注：「道以中庸為至；過雖若勝於不及，其失中則一也。」

【今譯】子貢問：「子張和子夏，那個好一點？」孔子說，「子張太過；子夏不及。」子貢說：「那麼是子張好一點囉？」孔子說：「太過和不及，同樣的不好！」

106

CHAI IS NAÏVE

GAO CHAI IS NAÏVE,

ZENGZI IS SLOW,

ZHUANSUN SHI IS BIASED,

AND ZHONG YOU IS HOT-TEMPERED.

YAN HUI SEEMS TO HAVE THE MOST PROMISE FOR SUCCESS; IT'S JUST THAT HE IS OFTEN HAMPERED BY POVERTY!

AND THEN THERE IS ZIGONG, WHO DOES BUSINESS INSTEAD OF RECEIVING INSTRUCTION. STILL, HE ONCE GUESSED RIGHT AT THE DIRECTION PRICES WOULD GO AND EARNED A LARGE SUM OF MONEY.

◉集解：「愚，愚直之愚。」

◉論語後案：「辟，偏也。」．

◉皇疏引王弼曰，「嗲，剛猛也。」

◉集解：「雖數空匱，而樂在其中矣！一曰，

屢，猶每也；空，猶虛心不能不知道。

◉貨殖，貨財生殖也。言子貢不如顏子之安貧

樂道。

◉焦循論語補疏：「賜能屢中，謂如其所憶度

而得贏餘也。」

107

BENEVOLENCE

WHAT IS BENEVOLENCE?

BENEVOLENCE IS OVERCOMING ONE'S SELFISH DESIRES AND ACTING IN ACCORDANCE WITH PROPRIETY.

IF YOU CAN DO THIS, EVERYONE WILL RECOGNIZE YOU AS BENEVOLENT. BENEVOLENCE COMES FROM ONESELF;

IT IS NOT SOMETHING OTHERS CAN GIVE TO YOU.

AND HOW, SPECIFICALLY, IS ONE TO ACT BENEVOLENTLY?

IF IT IS CONTRARY TO PROPRIETY, DO NOT LOOK AT IT.

IF IT IS CONTRARY TO PROPRIETY, DO NOT LISTEN TO IT.

IF IT IS CONTRARY TO PROPRIETY, DO NOT SAY IT.

IF IT IS CONTRARY TO PROPRIETY, DO NOT DO IT.

ALTHOUGH I'M NOT TOO BRIGHT, I HOPE THAT I CAN PRACTICE WHAT YOU'VE JUST SAID.

●復，有遵循故道的意義。所謂「知道」，乃指日常所應當履行的正道而言。禮，就是人們應當履行的正道。人們常因為情感衝動而偏離正道，便是違禮。一個人能夠常常控制自己的情感，避免違禮的事情，就是克己復禮。

●仁是孔門中最高的德行；顏淵是孔門中天資最高的學生。顏淵問仁，孔子教他「非禮勿視、非禮勿聽、非禮勿言、非禮勿動。」

108

## BROTHERS

ONE DAY WHEN CONFUCIUS' DISCIPLE SIMA NIU WAS QUITE DISTRAUGHT, HE ADDRESSED ZIXIA SAYING:

EVERYONE ELSE HAS BROTHERS, AND I SEEM TO BE THE ONLY ONE WHO DOESN'T!

SOMEONE ONCE SAID, "LIFE AND DEATH ARE DUE TO FATE; WEALTH AND POVERTY ARE ARRANGED BY HEAVEN."

IF A GENTLEMAN IS DEFERENTIAL AND CAUTIOUS, IF HE TREATS OTHERS WITH RESPECT AND PROPRIETY,

THEN EVERYONE WILL CONSIDER HIM HIS BROTHER.

HOW CAN A GENTLEMAN WORRY ABOUT NOT HAVING BROTHERS?

【今譯】司馬牛十分憂慮，說：「別人都有兄弟；我獨沒有！」子夏說：「我聽說：『一個人的死生是命定的；富貴也完全在於上天的安排。』一個君子對事謹敬而不出過錯，對人恭謙有禮，則天下人都可以成為兄弟的。你為什麼要愁沒有兄弟呢！」

◉亡音無。左哀十四年傳記宋桓魋作亂以及他的兄弟司馬牛為避亂而死於魯郭門外。

◉「死生」、「富貴」兩句，用以解司馬牛的「憂」。

109

## THE PEOPLE'S TRUST

ZIGONG ASKED CONFUCIUS ABOUT THE PRINCIPLES OF GOVERNING.

FOOD SHOULD BE SUFFICIENT, THE MILITARY SHOULD BE ADEQUATE, AND THE PEOPLE SHOULD TRUST THE GOVERNMENT.

IF NOT ALL OF THESE CAN BE MET, WHICH ONE IS MOST EXPENDABLE?

THE MILITARY.

AND OF THE REMAINING TWO, WHICH IS MOST EXPENDABLE?

THE FOOD.

EVER SINCE ANCIENT TIMES THERE HAVE BEEN WAR AND HUNGER, BUT IF A GOVERNMENT DOES NOT HOLD THE TRUST OF THE PEOPLE, IT WILL NOT LAST.

【今譯】子貢問為政的道理。孔子說:「充足糧食,充足軍備,人民對政府就有信心了。」子貢說:「如果迫於不得已,在糧食、軍備和人民的信心三者之中,一定要去掉一項,要先去那一項呢?」孔子說:「先去軍備。」子貢又說:「如果迫於不得已,在糧食和人民的信心二者之中,一定要去掉一項,又先去那一項呢?」孔子說:「去掉糧食。自古以來都有死亡,沒有糧食,也不過餓死;但如果人民對政府沒有信心,那國家也不能成立了。」

110

ASSIST IN THE GOOD

A GENTLEMAN ASSISTS OTHERS IN GOOD AND DOESN'T ASSIST IN BAD.

THIS MAN IS QUITE GOOD. EMPLOYING HIM WILL BE NO MISTAKE.

HE'S NOT BAD. IT WOULD BE WORTH IT TO WORK WITH HIM.

A LESSER MAN DOES THE OPPOSITE.

THAT GUY IS LOUSY. WHATEVER YOU DO, DON'T HIRE HIM.

HE'S HORRIBLE. DON'T WORK UNDER HIM.

【今譯】孔子說：「君子幫助別人做好事，不幫助別人做壞事。小人正好相反。」

●美，善也。

●穀梁隱元年傳：春秋成人之美，不成人之惡。

111

ZENGZI SAID:

A GENTLEMAN MAKES FRIENDS THROUGH HIS CULTURE;

AND THROUGH HIS FRIENDS, HE CULTIVATES HIS OWN BENEVOLENCE.

BENEVOLENCE

【今譯】曾子說：「君子用儀文來結交朋友；用朋友來助成自己的德行。」

●文，儀文；意同「禮貌」。

●用儀文益友；有益友；有了益友，就可以幫助我們為仁。

112

RECTIFYING ONESELF

IF ONE CAN RECTIFY ONE'S PERSON, WHAT PROBLEMS CAN THERE BE IN GOVERNING?

IF ONE CANNOT RECTIFY ONE'S PERSON, HOW CAN ONE RECTIFY OTHERS?

●本章申明「政者正也」的道理

【今譯】孔子說：「如果自己做得正，那對處理政治還有什麼難處？如果自己不正，那怎麼能够去正別人！」

113

# PATIENCE AND PRESCIENCE

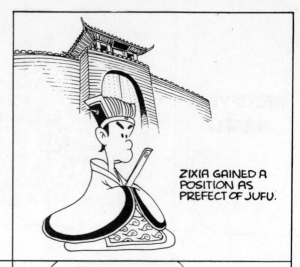

ZIXIA GAINED A POSITION AS PREFECT OF JUFU.

ONE DAY, HE ASKED CONFUCIUS ABOUT THE PRINCIPLES OF GOVERNING.

DO NOT HURRY SUCCESS; DO NOT FOCUS ON EXPEDIENCY.

IF YOU HURRY SUCCESS, YOU WILL FAIL IN YOUR DUTIES;

IF YOU FOCUS ON EXPEDIENCY, YOU WILL NOT ACCOMPLISH GREAT THINGS.

# GREED IS SHAMEFUL

YUAN XIAN ASKED CONFUCIUS ABOUT THE MEANING OF SHAME.

SHAME?

WHEN THE GOVERNMENT IS JUST, IT'S OKAY TO TAKE OFFICE AND RECEIVE A SALARY;

BUT TO DO THE SAME WHEN THE GOVERNMENT IS CORRUPT--

THIS IS SHAMEFUL!

◉ 穀，本義為粟，轉義為祿；現在叫「薪俸」。

◉ 泰伯篇：「子曰：邦有道，貧且賤焉，恥也；邦無道，富且貴焉，恥也！」

【今譯】原憲向孔子問「恥」的意義。孔子說：「國家政治清明，但知食祿而無所建樹；國家政治腐敗，仍然是做官食祿而無所建樹，這是可恥的。」

115

# THE COMPLETE PERSON

**WHAT IS A COMPLETE PERSON?**

SOMEONE WHO HAS THE INTELLIGENCE OF THE WISE OFFICIAL ZANG WUZHONG,

THE UNCOVETOUSNESS OF MENG GONGCHUO,

THE COURAGE OF ZHUANGZI OF BIAN,

AND THE TALENT OF RAN QIU,

TOGETHER WITH A KNOWLEDGE OF PROPRIETY AND MUSIC, CAN BE CONSIDERED COMPLETE.

BUT NOW WHEN WE SPEAK OF A COMPLETE PERSON, IT NEEDN'T BE THE SAME. IF ONE CAN JUST THINK OF WHAT'S RIGHT IN THE FACE OF TEMPTATION, SACRIFICE ONESELF IN THE FACE OF DANGER, AND HONOR PAST PROMISES, THIS PERSON CAN BE CONSIDERED COMPLETE!

●劉疏：「成人為成德之人。」

●臧武仲，魯大夫臧孫訖。知音智。

●荀子大略篇：「齊人欲伐魯；忌卞莊子，不敢過卞。」孔廣森疑卞莊子即孟莊子……「孟莊子有勇名；或嘗食采於卞，因以為號。楚語

●孔曰：「久要，舊約也。」

……魯有弁費。謂孟孫季孫也。弁卞一字。

●集注：「平生，平日也。」

116

SAYING AND DOING

IF ONE'S SPEAKING OF SOMETHING IS IMMODEST, HIS CARRYING IT OUT WILL BE DIFFICULT!

【今譯】孔子說：「一個人説大話而不會慚愧的人，要他脚踏實地去做事，是很困難的！」

●馬曰：「怍，慙也。內有其實，則言之不怍。積其實者，為之難也！」

117

EXTRAVAGANT
IN DEEDS

A GENTLEMAN
IS MODEST IN
WORDS

I'LL
DO MY
BEST.

AND EXTRAVAGANT
IN DEEDS.

HE
DOES A LOT,
AND HE DOES
IT WELL.

●禮記雜記：「有其言而無其行，君子恥也。」
●「而」在此作「之」解。
●表記：「君子恥有其辭而無其德；有其德而無其行。」

【今譯】孔子說：「君子應以言過於行為可恥。」

118

# THROWING STONES

ZIGONG LIKED TO CRITICIZE THE FAULTS OF OTHERS.

HA HA HA HA

ZIGONG! ARE YOU, YOURSELF, PERFECT?

!

AS FOR ME, I DON'T HAVE THE TIME TO GO AROUND CRITICIZING OTHERS!

●釋文：「方人，鄭本作謗，謂言人之過惡。」

●夫音符。「謗人」近於「言人之不善」，所以孔
子微諷子貢。（皇本作「賜也賢乎我哉，
我則不暇。」正平本作「賜也賢乎我夫！我
則不暇。」阮記以兩本「皆非」。）

【今譯】子貢批評別人的不對。孔子說：「賜真能幹！我就沒有這種閒工夫！」

119

【今譯】孔子說：「驥的所以稱為驥，不僅因為牠能日行千里，更因為牠有馴良的德性。」

●太平御覽引鄭注：「驥，古之善馬。」說文：「驥，千里馬也。」

●鄭曰：「德者，調良之謂。」調良即馴服和善之意。

A GOOD HORSE

A GOOD HORSE IS PRAISED NOT FOR ITS STRENGTH,

BUT FOR ITS VIRTUE.

## HOW TO TREAT ONE'S ENEMIES

CONFUCIUS WAS ONCE ASKED:

SHOULD I REPAY AN ENEMY WITH KINDNESS?

IF YOU REPAY AN ENEMY WITH KINDNESS, HOW WILL YOU REPAY SOMEONE WHO IS KIND TO YOU?

YOU SHOULD TREAT AN ENEMY WITH DECENCY AND FAIRNESS;

AND YOU SHOULD REPAY KINDNESS WITH KINDNESS.

●廣雅釋言：報，復也。玉篇：報，酬也，答也。

●老子六十三篇：「報怨以德。」

●禮記表記：「子曰：以德報德，則民有所勸；以怨報怨，則民有所懲。」

【今譯】有人説：「用德來報怨：你看怎麼樣？」孔子回答道：「那麼用什麼來報『德』呢！我們可以用正直的行為來報『怨』；用德來報『德』。」

121

【今譯】孔子說：「沒有人能夠了解我罷！」子貢說：「為什麼沒有人能夠了解老師？」孔子說：「不恨天、不怪人；從平常的事情思考起，逐漸進到高明的境界。恐怕只有天會知道我罷！」

# UNDERSTANDING CONFUCIUS

NO ONE UNDERSTANDS ME!

HOW COME NO ONE UNDERSTANDS YOU, MASTER?

I BEAR NO GRUDGE AGAINST HEAVEN, AND I DO NOT BLAME OTHERS. I LEARN FROM THE AFFAIRS OF PEOPLE,

PERHAPS THE ONLY ONE WHO UNDERSTANDS ME IS HEAVEN!

APPLYING MYSELF TO SIMPLE THINGS AT HAND, AND I GRADUALLY UNDERSTAND THE PRINCIPLES OF HEAVEN.

122

STUBBORN

ZHONG YOU ONCE PUT UP FOR THE NIGHT OUTSIDE OF SHIMEN IN QI.

EXCUSE ME.

OH, YOU MEAN THE ONE WHO KNOWS HE WON'T SUCCEED BUT KEEPS ON ANYWAY?

WHERE ARE YOU FROM?

I COME FROM THE HOUSE OF CONFUCIUS.

【今譯】子路在石門宿了一夜。管門的人問他：「你是那裏來的？」子路說：「從孔家來。」管門的人說：「就是那位明知做不成還要去做的先生嗎？」

◉鄭注：「晨門，主晨夜開閉也。」

◉劉疏：「子路時自魯外出，晚宿石門也。」

123

## A WASTED LIFE

ONCE WHEN CONFUCIUS' OLD ACQUAINTANCE YUAN RANG SAW CONFUCIUS COMING, HE DISRESPECTFULLY CROUCHED DOWN AND WAITED FOR HIM.

WHEN YOU WERE YOUNG, YOU DIDN'T UNDERSTAND HUMILITY OR RESPECT FOR ELDERS.

AS AN ADULT YOU HAD NO ACCOMPLISHMENTS;

AND NOW YOU'RE OLD AND REFUSE TO DIE. WHAT A DISGRACE!

WITH THIS, HE RAPPED THE MAN ON THE SHIN WITH HIS CANE.

WHACK

●禮記檀弓下：「孔子之故人曰原壤。其母死，

　夫子助之沐槨。」

●夷，箕踞；俟，等待。

●賊，意同「禍害」。

●叩，敂之簡體。說文：「敂，擊也：讀若扣。」

【今譯】原壤伸展兩腿蹲坐著等孔子。孔子說：「年幼時不懂禮貌；長大後也沒什麼表現；老了還不死：真是禍害！」就用手杖敲他的腳脛。

124

# CONDITIONAL SERVICE

SHI YU CERTAINLY IS AN UPRIGHT AND STRAIGHTFORWARD PERSON! WHEN THE GOVERNMENT IS JUST, HE DUTIFULLY TAKES HIS POSITION. HE'S AS STRAIGHT AS AN ARROW.

WHEN THE GOVERNMENT IS CORRUPT, HE TELLS IT LIKE IT IS! HE'S AS STRAIGHT AS AN ARROW.

QU BOYU CERTAINLY IS A GENTLEMAN! WHEN THE GOVERNMENT IS JUST, HE WORKS AS A MINISTER,

AND WHEN THE GOVERNMENT IS CORRUPT, HE CONCEALS HIS TALENTS AND GOES OFF BY HIMSELF.

◉泰伯篇：「天下有道則見，無道則隱。」

◉鄭注：「史魚，衛大夫，名鰌。」
◉集注：「卷，收也。懷，藏也。」

【今譯】孔子說：「史魚真是正直！國政清明，他和矢一樣直；國政混亂，他也和矢一樣直！蘧伯玉真是個君子！國政清明，他就出來做事；國政昏亂，他也可以收藏自己的才能！」

125

【今譯】子貢問「為仁」的方法。孔子說：「工匠要做好他的工作，必須先把他的工具弄好。在一個國家裏，我們應該在賢能的官吏下做事，應該結交有仁德的人士。」

◉劉疏：「為，猶行也。」

◉必先利其器，比喻為仁須先有為仁的利器，為仁的利器，既是「大夫之賢者」和「士之仁者」。

CULTIVATING BENEVOLENCE

ZIGONG ASKED CONFUCIUS HOW TO CULTIVATE BENEVOLENCE IN ONESELF.

BEFORE AN ARTISAN DOES HIS JOB, HE MUST ALWAYS GRIND HIS TOOLS FIRST.

LIVING IN ANY COUNTRY, ONE SHOULD SERVE UNDER A CAPABLE AND VIRTUOUS MINISTER

AND MAKE FRIENDS WITH BENEVOLENT OFFICERS.

126

THINKING AHEAD

IN ANY MATTER, IF ONE DOESN'T THINK FAR INTO THE FUTURE,

TROUBLE WILL BE NEAR AT HAND.

◎「遠慮」，即「周密的思慮」。

◎「近憂」，隨時可能發生的憂患。遠近二字，非指距離而言。

【今譯】孔子說：「一個人對自己的行為如果沒有周密的思慮，那麼，他就隨時會有憂患的來臨。」

127

## THE GOLDEN RULE

IS THERE ONE WORD THAT CAN ACT AS A STANDARD OF CONDUCT FOR ONE'S WHOLE LIFE?

PERHAPS IT WOULD BE "THOUGHTFULNESS."

WHAT YOU, YOURSELF, DO NOT LIKE,

DO NOT IMPOSE ON OTHERS.

【今譯】子貢問道：「有沒有一個字可以讓我們一生照著做的？」孔子説：「該是『恕』字吧！自己不喜歡的事情，不要加在別人身上！」

●「一言」，即「一個字」。
●里仁篇：「子曰：吾道一以貫之。曾子曰：夫子之道，忠恕而已矣！」
●中庸：「忠恕違道不遠：施諸己而不願，亦勿施於人。」

THINKING VS. STUDYING

IN THE PAST, I HAVE GONE ALL DAY WITHOUT EATING,

GONE ALL NIGHT WITHOUT SLEEPING...

AND SPENT ALL MY TIME THINKING; BUT TO NO AVAIL.

IT IS BETTER TO STUDY.

◉大戴禮勸學篇：「孔子曰：吾嘗終日而思矣；不如須臾之所學也。」

◉為政篇：「子曰，學而不思則罔；思而不學則殆。」講究學和思應並重。

◉此處的「思」，是「思而不學」的「思」。

【今譯】孔子說：「我曾經整天不吃、終夜不睡，而去苦思，卻徒勞無功；還不如學的好！」

129

YIELD TO NO ONE

WHEN AN OPPORTUNITY TO PRACTICE BENEVOLENCE ARISES,

DO NOT YIELD EVEN TO YOUR TEACHER.

EXCUSE ME! BUT I BELIEVE I CAN HANDLE THIS MATTER OF BENEVOLENCE!

●孔曰，「當行仁之事不復讓於師，言行仁急。」

●集注：「當仁，以仁為己任也。」
●集注：「雖師亦無所遜，言當勇往而必為也。」

【今譯】孔子說：「遇到行仁時，對於老師也不必有所遜讓。」

130

THE THREE TEMPTATIONS

THERE ARE THREE THINGS A GENTLEMAN MUST ABSTAIN FROM: IN YOUTH, WHEN THE VITAL FLUIDS HAVE YET TO STABILIZE, THE ABSTENTION IS LUST.

IN MIDDLE AGE, WHEN THE VITAL FLUIDS ARE FULLY POTENT, THE ABSTENTION IS CONTENTIOUSNESS.

IN OLD AGE, WHEN THE VITAL FLUIDS HAVE SUBSIDED, THE ABSTENTION IS ACQUISITIVENESS.

●淮南詮言訓：「凡人之性，少則猖狂，壯則彊暴，老則好利。」

●少，詩照切。
●此孔子教人應隨時「慎行」也。
【今譯】孔子説：「君子有三件事要戒慎：年輕時血氣未定，要戒的是女色；到了壯年，血氣正旺，要戒的是好勇鬥狠；到了老年，血氣已衰，要戒的是貪得無厭。」

131

**THE NINE CONSIDERATIONS**

THERE ARE NINE CONSIDERATIONS A GENTLEMAN SHOULD KEEP IN MIND:

WHEN LOOKING, BE MINDFUL OF CLARITY,

WHEN LISTENING, BE MINDFUL OF ACUITY, acute discriminating to detail

FOR FACIAL EXPRESSIONS, BE MINDFUL OF GENIALITY,

FOR DEMEANOR, BE MINDFUL OF DEFERENCE, yield to another's opinion

BE SINCERE... WHEN SPEAKING, BE MINDFUL OF SINCERITY.

WHEN ACTING, BE MINDFUL OF REVERENCE,

WHEN CONFUSED, BE MINDFUL OF INQUIRING,

WHEN ANGRY, BE MINDFUL OF THE CONSEQUENCES,

WHEN SEEING THE CHANCE FOR GAIN, BE MINDFUL OF WHAT IS RIGHT.

●君子有九項應該留心思考的事：看的時候想要看分明，聽的時候想要聽得清楚，與人相處，臉色想要溫和，待人時的容貌態度想要謙遜，平日說話想要忠信，處理一切事情應該要小心謹慎，有所疑惑便要問人，難是患難。胸懷忿怒，便要想到可能由此會發生許多的患難，見到了有利可圖，要想到是不是合於義理。

132

**PRAISING DEEDS**

A PASSAGE FROM THE *BOOK OF SONGS* SAYS THAT PEOPLE AREN'T PRAISED FOR THEIR WEALTH BUT FOR THEIR EXTRAORDINARY ACTIONS.

DUKE JING OF QI HAD FOUR THOUSAND HORSES, BUT WHEN HE DIED, THE PEOPLE FELT NO REASON TO PRAISE HIM.

ON THE OTHER HAND, ALTHOUGH BOYI AND SHUQI (BROTHERS WHO REFUSED THE CROWN OUT OF PRINCIPLE) STARVED TO DEATH AT THE FOOT OF SHOUYANG MOUNTAIN, PEOPLE PRAISE THEM EVEN NOW. DO NOT THE LINES

PRAISE STEMS NOT FROM PROSPERITY, AND ONLY FROM THE EXTRAORDINARY

REFER TO THIS?

【今譯】「齊景公有馬四千匹；他死的時候，老百姓並不覺得他有什麼值得稱述的善行。詩經上說『誠不以富，亦祇以異。』就是說這種情形吧！」伯夷、叔齊在首陽山下挨餓，人們到現在還稱讚他們。

133

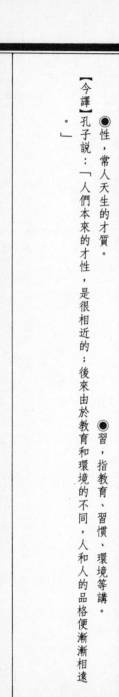

【今譯】孔子說：「人們本來的才性，是很相近的；後來由於教育和環境的不同，人和人的品格便漸漸相遠。」

●性，常人天生的才質。

●習，指教育、習慣、環境等講。

NATURE VS. NURTURE

PEOPLE'S ORIGINAL NATURES ARE NEARLY THE SAME,

BUT DUE TO DIFFERENT EDUCATIONS AND ENVIRONMENTS,

THEY GROW FURTHER AND FURTHER APART.

134

# THE SIX DEFECTS

ZHONG YOU, HAVE YOU HEARD ABOUT HOW THE SIX VIRTUES CAN BECOME THE SIX DEFECTS?

NO, I HAVEN'T.

SIT DOWN AND I'LL TELL YOU.

YES, MASTER.

TO LOVE BENEVOLENCE BUT NOT LOVE LEARNING IS TO SLIP INTO FOOLISHNESS;

TO LOVE WISDOM BUT NOT LOVE LEARNING IS TO SLIP INTO VAGARIES;

TO LOVE SINCERITY BUT NOT LOVE LEARNING IS TO ENCOUNTER HARM;

TO LOVE FORTHRIGHTNESS BUT NOT LOVE LEARNING IS TO BECOME RASH;

TO LOVE COURAGE BUT NOT LOVE LEARNING IS TO INVITE DISASTER;

TO LOVE STRENGTH BUT NOT LOVE LEARNING IS TO BECOME WILD.

●女音汝；六言，即仁、知、信、直、勇、剛
六事。這六事是美德；但如果只有美德而不
加求學問，就可能有愚、蕩、賊、絞、亂、
狂的弊病。

●語，魚據切。

●泰伯篇：「子曰：恭而無禮則勞；慎而無禮
則葸；勇而無禮則亂；直而無禮則絞。」

135

【今譯】孔子說：「外表威嚴而內心軟弱的人，這種欺世盜名之輩，若用小民來做比喻，就和竊賊一樣！」

◎ 集注：「厲，威嚴也。荏，柔弱也。」

◎ 三蒼：「窬，門邊小竇也。」「穿窬」，意為「挖孔」；「穿窬之盜」，即「挖牆的竊賊」。

THE BRAZEN BURGLAR

A PERSON WHO PUTS ON BRAZEN AIRS,

WHILE BEING COWARDLY ON THE INSIDE,

IF WE DRAW A COMPARISON FROM LESSER MEN,

IS LIKE THE SHAMELESS BURGLAR THAT DIGS A HOLE OR SCALES A WALL.

# CONFUCIUS AND RU BEI

RU BEI WENT TO SEE CONFUCIUS...

YES, MASTER.

TELL HIM THAT I'M ILL AND CAN'T SEE HIM.

SORRY, BUT MY TEACHER IS ILL AND CAN'T SEE YOU.

THEN CONFUCIUS TOOK UP HIS ZITHER AND INTENTIONALLY PLAYED AND SANG SO LOUD THAT RU BEI COULD HEAR HIM.

THAT SCOUNDREL! HE ISN'T SICK AT ALL.

◎集解：「孺悲，魯人也。」
◉御覽引韓詩外傳云：「子路曰，聞之於夫子：士不中間而見，女無媒而嫁者，非君子之行也。」

◉鄭注云：「將命，傳辭者。」戶，室戶也。

137

PLAYING GAMES

SOMEONE WHO, HAVING EATEN HIS FILL, GOES ABOUT ALL DAY WITHOUT USING HIS MIND AT ALL...

WILL HAVE DIFFICULTY EVER ACCOMPLISHING ANYTHING.

AREN'T THERE THOSE WHO PLAY GAMES ALL DAY? THIS IS STILL BETTER THAN NOT USING YOUR MIND AT ALL!

◉衛靈公「羣居終日」章鄭注：「難矣哉，言無所成。」

◉焦循孟子正義：「博，蓋即今之雙陸。奕為圍棋之專名，與博同類而異事。」

【今譯】孔子說：「整天吃飽飯，一點也不用心思：這種生活是很難有所成就的。不是有玩雙陸和下圍棋的人麼？就做這些事情，也比整天不用一點心思還要好些！」

138

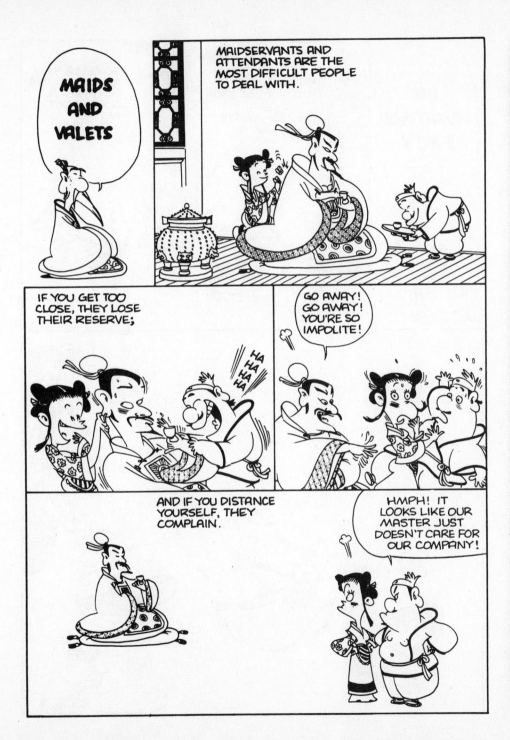

MAIDS AND VALETS

MAIDSERVANTS AND ATTENDANTS ARE THE MOST DIFFICULT PEOPLE TO DEAL WITH.

IF YOU GET TOO CLOSE, THEY LOSE THEIR RESERVE;

HA HA HA HA

GO AWAY! GO AWAY! YOU'RE SO IMPOLITE!

AND IF YOU DISTANCE YOURSELF, THEY COMPLAIN.

HMPH! IT LOOKS LIKE OUR MASTER JUST DOESN'T CARE FOR OUR COMPANY!

【今譯】孔子說：「家中的婢僕是最難以相處的：接近他們就對你不恭；疏遠他們，他們又會怨恨你。」

◉這裡的女子、小人，是專指婢妾僕隸等類人。

◉近、孫、遠都去聲。

139

【今譯】孔子說：「一個人到了四十歲時還顯現惡行，這一生大概也就做不出什麼好事了！」

●見，音現；惡，如字。

AN IMMATURE FORTY

TAKE THAT!

SOMEONE WHO IS FORTY YEARS OLD AND STILL GOES ABOUT ACTING WICKEDLY...

WILL NEVER DO A SINGLE DECENT THING HIS WHOLE LIFE!

140

## BENEVOLENCE AND DUTY

THE INFAMOUS LAST EMPEROR OF THE SHANG DYNASTY WAS A HORRIBLE AND DEPRAVED TYRANT. BECAUSE OF THIS, HIS BROTHER, THE VISCOUNT OF WEI, LEFT HIM;

AND ANOTHER UNCLE NAMED BIGAN ADMONISHED HIM REPEATEDLY AND WAS FINALLY EVISCERATED.

HIS UNCLE, THE VISCOUNT OF JI, WAS LOCKED UP AND MADE A SLAVE BECAUSE HE DARED TO ADMONISH HIM;

APPROVING OF THESE MEN'S CONDUCT, CONFUCIUS SAID:

THE SHANG DYNASTY HAD THREE BENEVOLENT MEN!

●史記殷本紀：「帝乙長子曰微子啓；啓母賤，不得嗣。帝乙崩，子辛立；天下謂之紂。帝紂好酒淫樂，厚賦稅；百姓怨望。西伯卒，紂愈淫亂不止。微子數諫，不聽；遂去。

比干乃強諫紂。紂怒，曰，『吾聞聖人心有七竅。』剖比干觀其心。箕子懼，乃詳狂為奴；紂又囚之。」

【今譯】微子離開了殷紂；箕子做了奴隸；比干因強諫而被殺。孔子説：「殷有三個仁人！」

141

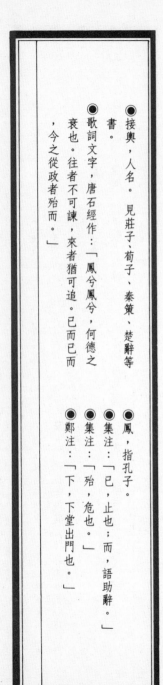

●接輿，人名。見莊子、荀子、秦策、楚辭等書。

●歌詞文字，唐石經作：「鳳兮鳳兮，何德之衰也。往者不可諫，來者猶可追。已而已而，今之從政者殆而。」

●鳳，指孔子。

●集注：「已，止也；而，語助辭。」

●集注：「殆，危也。」

●鄭注：「下，下堂出門也。」

# CRAZY JIEYU

A MAN FROM CHU NAMED JIEYU, WHO PRETENDED TO BE CRAZY TO AVOID GOVERNMENT SERVICE, PASSED BY CONFUCIUS ONE DAY SINGING A SONG:

OH, PHOENIX! OH, PHOENIX! HOW VIRTUE HAS DECLINED! YOU CAN'T GET BACK THE PAST, BUT YOU CAN STILL CATCH UP WITH THE FUTURE...

FORGET IT! FORGET IT! BEING AN OFFICIAL NOW IS ALL TOO DANGEROUS!

CONFUCIUS DESCENDED FROM HIS CARRIAGE HOPING TO TALK WITH JIEYU. JIEYU, HOWEVER, QUICKLY DEPARTED THE AREA BEFORE CONFUCIUS COULD SAY ANYTHING.

# THE TWO RECLUSES

ONE DAY WHEN THE TWO RECLUSES CHANG JU AND JIE NI WERE OUT WORKING THEIR FIELDS, CONFUCIUS HAPPENED TO PASS BY.

GO ASK THEM WHERE WE CAN CROSS THE RIVER?

YES, MASTER.

COULD YOU PLEASE TELL ME WHERE WE MAY CROSS THE RIVER?

WHO IS THAT IN THE CARRIAGE HOLDING THE REINS?

◉ 鄭曰：「長沮、桀溺，隱者也。」耦而耕，是二人併力發土的意思。

◉ 説文：「津，水渡也。」

◉ 皇疏：「執輿；猶執轡也。」子路本在車上執轡；現在下車問津，孔子代為執轡。

◉ 漢書敍傳顏注：「避人之士，謂孔子；避世之士，溺自謂也。」

143

【今譯】長沮、桀溺在一起耕田。孔子路過，叫子路向他們問過渡的地方。長沮說：「那執轡的是誰？」子路說：「是孔丘。」長沮說：「是魯國的孔丘麼？」子路說：「是！」長沮說：「那他一定知道過渡的地方了！」子路向桀溺問。桀溺說：「你是誰？」子路說：「是仲由。」桀溺說：「是魯國孔丘的門

● 鄭曰，「耰，覆種也。輟，止也。」
● 「與易」的與，義同為。

144

WITH EVERY PLACE IN THE WORLD IN CHAOS, WHO IS THERE THAT CAN CHANGE ANYTHING FOR THE BETTER?

IT SEEMS TO ME THAT INSTEAD OF FOLLOWING THAT MAN WHO AVOIDS WICKED MEN, YOU WOULD BE BETTER OFF FOLLOWING MEN LIKE US WHO AVOID THE CHAOTIC WORLD.

AFTER SPEAKING, HE CONTINUED HIS WORK IN THE FIELD.

ZHONG YOU RETURNED AND TOLD CONFUCIUS WHAT THEY HAD SAID.

WE CANNOT LIVE WITH THE BIRDS AND THE BEASTS, SO IF WE DON'T LIVE WITH PEOPLE, WHOM SHALL WE LIVE WITH?

IF THE WORLD WERE PEACEFUL AND HARMONIOUS, I WOULDN'T NEED TO CHANGE ANYTHING.

徒嗎?」子路答道:「是的。」桀溺說:「天下到處都是一樣的混亂;有誰能來變易它呢?我看你與其跟隨那逃避壞人的人,還不如跟隨我們這些逃避亂世的人!」說完了繼續耰田。孔子悵然;說道:「我們不能和鳥獸在一起生活;我們不和人類在一起、更和什麼在一起呢!如果天下太平,我就不會來變易它了。」話告訴孔子。孔子悵然;說道:「我們不能和鳥獸在一起生活;我們不和人類在一起、更和什麼在一起呢!如果天下太平,我就不會來變易它了。」

145

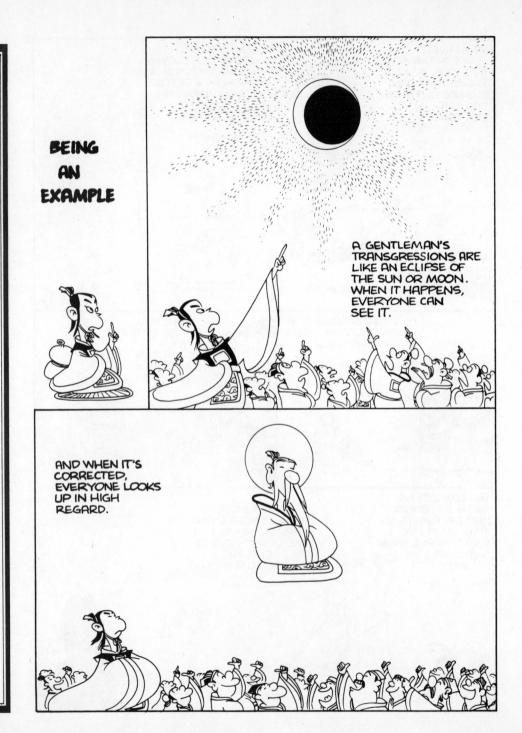

BEING AN EXAMPLE

A GENTLEMAN'S TRANSGRESSIONS ARE LIKE AN ECLIPSE OF THE SUN OR MOON. WHEN IT HAPPENS, EVERYONE CAN SEE IT.

AND WHEN IT'S CORRECTED, EVERYONE LOOKS UP IN HIGH REGARD.

●因為君子不會文過（掩飾自己的過失），所以大家都能看見他的過失。

●説文：「更，改也。」

●皇疏：「日月蝕罷，改闇更明，則天下皆瞻仰。君子之德，亦不以先過為累也。」

【今譯】子貢說：「君子的過失，就像日蝕月蝕一樣：他有過失，大家都能看見；他改過了，大家仍然瞻仰他。」

146

# The Disciples of Confucius

(FROM SIMA QIAN'S *THE HISTORIAN'S RECORDS*)

孔子之所嚴事：於周則老子；於衞，蘧伯玉；於齊，晏平仲；於楚，老萊子；於鄭，子產；於魯，孟公綽。數稱臧文仲、柳下惠、銅鞮伯華、介山子然，孔子皆後之，不並世。

147

OF MY STUDENTS, THERE ARE SEVENTY-SEVEN WHO ARE WELL VERSED IN THE ARTS, AND EACH OF THEM HAS HIS OWN ACCOMPLISHMENTS.

THOSE WHOSE STRENGTH LIES IN GOVERNING ARE RAN YOU AND ZHONG YOU.

THOSE WHOSE STRENGTH LIES IN VIRTUOUS CONDUCT ARE YAN HUI, MIN SUN, RAN BONIU, AND RAN YONG.

THOSE WHOSE STRENGTH LIES IN SPEAKING ARE ZAI YU AND ZIGONG.

AND THOSE WHOSE STRENGTH LIES IN CULTURE AND LEARNING ARE ZIYOU AND ZIXIA.

孔子曰「受業身通者七十有七人」，皆異能之士也。德行：顏淵，閔子騫，冉伯牛，仲弓。政事：冉有，季路。言語：宰我，子貢。文學：子游，子夏。師也辟，參也魯，柴也愚，由也喭，回也屢空。賜不受命而貨殖焉，億則屢中。

148

SURNAME: YAN

GIVEN NAME: HUI

COMING-OF-AGE NAME: ZIYUAN

HOME STATE: LU

YEARS YOUNGER THAN CONFUCIUS: THIRTY

AT THE AGE OF TWENTY-NINE, YAN HUI'S HAIR HAD ALREADY TURNED WHITE, AND HE PASSED AWAY WHEN HE WAS ONLY THIRTY-TWO. AT HIS DEATH, CONFUCIUS WEPT WITH MOMENTOUS GRIEF.

MASTER... PLEASE... TRY NOT TO FEEL SO BAD...

OH, MY! I'LL NEVER BE ABLE TO TRANSMIT THE WAY! I'M FINISHED! I'M FINISHED!

AM I REALLY GRIEVING TOO MUCH? IF I DON'T GRIEVE FOR HIM, WHO ELSE IS WORTH GRIEVING FOR?

顏回者，魯人也，字子淵。少孔子三十歲。顏淵問仁孔子曰：「克己復禮，天下歸仁焉。」孔子曰：「賢哉回也！一簞食，一瓢飲，在陋巷，人不堪其憂，回也不改其樂。」「回也如愚；退而省其私，亦足以發，回也不愚。」「用之則行，捨之則藏，唯我與爾有是夫！」回年二十九，髮盡白蚤死。孔子哭之慟，曰：「自吾有回，門人益親。」魯哀公問：「弟子孰為好學。」孔子對曰：「有顏回者好學，不遷怒，不貳過。不幸短命死矣，今也則亡。」

149

**SURNAME:** MIN
**GIVEN NAME:** SUN
**COMING-OF-AGE NAME:** ZIQIAN
**HOME STATE:** LU
**YEARS YOUNGER THAN CONFUCIUS:** FIFTEEN

CONFUCIUS PRAISED MIN SUN, SAYING: "MIN SUN CERTAINLY PRACTICES FILIAL VIRTUE! HE SERVES HIS PARENTS AND LOVES HIS BROTHERS.

"NOBODY HAS ANYTHING BUT PRAISE FOR HOW HE TREATS HIS PARENTS AND BROTHERS."

HE HAD GREAT SELF-RESPECT AND INTEGRITY. HE DIDN'T SERVE AS HOUSEHOLD MINISTER UNDER POWERFUL OFFICIALS, NOR DID HE ACCEPT EMOLUMENTS FROM FOREIGN NOBLES. IT IS FOR THESE REASONS THAT HE SAID TO AN INSISTENT FOREIGN EMISSARY:

IF YOU COME LOOKING FOR ME AGAIN, I'LL BE FORCED TO CROSS THE WEN RIVER AND LEAVE THE COUNTRY ALTOGETHER.

閔損字子騫。少孔子十五歲。

孔子曰：「孝哉閔子騫！人不閒於其父母昆弟之言。」不仕大夫，不食汙君之祿。「如有復我者，必在汶上矣。」

●閔子騫是孔子的學生，其母死，父更娶，復生二子。後母因虐待閔子騫，其父察知，甚怒，欲逐後母，子騫婉言懇留，父母均受感化，終得相安無事，所以孔子稱讚他。

150

SURNAME: RAN

GIVEN NAME: YONG

COMING-OF-AGE NAME: ZHONGGONG

HOME STATE: LU

YEARS YOUNGER THAN CONFUCIUS: TWENTY-NINE

CAME FROM A LOWER-CLASS FAMILY

EVEN THOUGH IT IS MERELY THE OFFSPRING OF A PLOW OX, AS LONG AS IT HAS A PURE CINNABAR COAT AND ITS HORNS ARE SYMMETRICAL, IT IS QUALIFIED TO BE USED IN A SACRIFICIAL CEREMONY.

AND ALTHOUGH SOMEONE MAY OBJECT DUE TO ITS HUMBLE ORIGINS,

WOULD THE GODS OF THE MOUNTAINS AND RIVERS EVER REFUSE SUCH AN OFFERING?

冉雍字仲弓。

仲弓問政，孔子曰：「出門如見大賓，使民如承大祭。在邦無怨，在家無怨。」

孔子以仲弓為有德行，曰：「雍也可使南面。」

仲弓父，賤人。孔子曰：「犁牛之子騂且角，雖欲勿用，山川其舍諸？」

151

仲由字子路，卞人也。少孔子九歲。子路性鄙，好勇力，志伉直，冠雄雞，佩豭豚，陵暴孔子。孔子設禮稍誘子路，子路後儒服委質，因門人請為弟子。子路問政，孔子曰：「先之勞之。」請益。曰：「無倦。」（下略）

孔子曰：「片言可以折獄者，其由也與！」「由也好勇過我，無所取材。」「若由也，不得其死然。」「衣敝縕袍與衣狐貉者立而不恥者，其由也與！」「由也升堂矣，未入於室也。」

**SURNAME:** ZHONG
**GIVEN NAME:** YOU
**COMING-OF-AGE NAME:** ZILU
**HOME STATE:** LU, BIAN COUNTY
**YEARS YOUNGER THAN CONFUCIUS:** NINE

WITH AN INFLAMMATORY AND STRAIGHTFORWARD CHARACTER, HE WAS ORIGINALLY A COARSE AND UNREFINED MAN WHO ENJOYED FIGHTING AND EXHIBITING HIS BRAVERY. HE WAS TRANSFORMED BY CONFUCIUS. IN HIS LATER YEARS, HE HELD THE POSITION OF CHIEF MAGISTRATE OF THE CITY OF PU IN WEI. HE WAS KILLED DURING A REBELLION THAT SWEPT THROUGH WEI.

TO WEAR WORN CLOTHES AND STAND NEXT TO SOMEONE WEARING FURS AND LEATHER YET NOT FEEL THE LEAST BIT ASHAMED--I'M AFRAID ONLY ZHONG YOU WOULD BE CAPABLE OF THAT!

ZHONG YOU'S STUDIES HAVE ACHIEVED A CERTAIN LEVEL OF ENLIGHTENMENT; IT'S JUST THAT THEY HAVE YET TO ATTAIN THAT REALM OF PROFUNDITY.

**SURNAME:** ZAI
**GIVEN NAME:** YU
**COMING-OF-AGE NAME:** ZIWO
**HOME STATE:** LU
**AGE DIFFERENCE WITH CONFUCIUS:** UNKNOWN

WITH A SHARP TONGUE AND QUICK WIT, THIS MAN WAS A FINE SPEAKER AND A GOOD DEBATER. ZAI YU HELD THE POSITION OF CHIEF MAGISTRATE OF LINZI, BUT BECAUSE HE PARTICIPATED IN THE TIAN CHANG UPRISING, HE AND HIS ENTIRE FAMILY WERE DESTROYED. HE ALSO LOST FAVOR WITH CONFUCIUS.

HELP!

SUPPOSE THAT A BENEVOLENT MAN WERE TOLD THAT A PERSON HAD FALLEN IN A WELL, SHOULD HE JUMP IN TO SAVE HIM?

WHY SHOULD HE DO THAT? A GENTLEMAN WOULD GO TO THE SIDE OF THE WELL TO SAVE HIM, BUT HE WOULDN'T JUMP IN.

A GENTLEMAN CAN BE DECEIVED, BUT HE CANNOT BE BLINDED BY CIRCUMSTANCE.

宰予字子我。利口辯辭。既受業，問：「三年之喪不已久乎？君子三年不為禮，禮必壞；三年不為樂，樂必崩。舊穀既沒，新穀既升，鑽燧改火，期可已矣。」子曰：「食夫稻，衣夫錦，於汝安乎？」曰：「安。」「汝安則為之。君子居喪，食旨不甘，聞樂不樂，故弗為也。」宰我出，子曰：「予之不仁也！子生三年然後免於父母之懷。夫三年之喪，天下之通義也。」

153

SURNAME: DUANMU
GIVEN NAME: SI
COMING-OF-AGE NAME: ZIGONG
HOME STATE: WEI
YEARS YOUNGER THAN CONFUCIUS: THIRTY-ONE

A FINE SPEAKER, AND A GOOD DEBATER, HE ENJOYED PRAISING OTHER PEOPLE'S MERITS, BUT AT THE SAME TIME, HE WOULD NOT IGNORE THEIR TRANSGRESSIONS. MORE THAN ONCE HE HELPED LU AND WEI RESOLVE STALE-MATES. HE CAME FROM A WEALTHY FAMILY, AND BEING GOOD AT BUSINESS, HE BUILT UP RICHES OF A THOUSAND GOLD PIECES. HE DIED LATE IN THE STATE OF QI.

MASTER, WHAT DO YOU THINK OF ME?

YOU ARE LIKE A USEFUL IMPLEMENT.

LIKE WHAT KIND OF IMPLEMENT?

YOU ARE LIKE THE RICHLY ADORNED HU-LIAN SACRIFICIAL VESSEL IN THE ROYAL ANCESTRAL TEMPLE!

端沐賜，衞人，字子貢。少孔子三十一歲。

子貢利口巧辭，孔子常黜其辯。問曰：「汝與回也孰愈？」對曰：「賜也何敢望回！回也聞一以知十，賜也聞一以知二。」

子貢既已受業，問曰：「賜何人也？」孔子曰：「汝器也。」曰：「何器也？」曰：「瑚璉也。」

154

**SURNAME:** PU
**GIVEN NAME:** SHANG
**COMING-OF-AGE NAME:** ZIXIA
**HOME STATE:** WEI, WEN REGION
**YEARS YOUNGER THAN CONFUCIUS:** FORTY-FIVE

AFTER CONFUCIUS DIED, ZIXIA TOOK UP RESIDENCE IN THE XIHE REGION OF WEI, WHERE HE BEGAN TEACHING AND ATTRACTING FOLLOWERS OF HIS OWN. HE ALSO BECAME THE PERSONAL TUTOR TO MARQUIS WEN OF WEI. HIS SON DIED YOUNG, AND HIS GRIEF OVER IT CAUSED HIM TO CRY HIMSELF BLIND.

IN THE ANCIENT SONGS IT SAYS:
LOVELY SMILE AND CHEEKS WHITE,
BEAUTIFUL EYES CLEAR AND BRIGHT,
PLAINNESS MAKES THE PATTERN RIGHT
WHAT DO THESE THREE LINES MEAN?

THEY MEAN THAT WHEN YOU PAINT, YOU FIRST PREPARE A PLAIN GROUND, AND THEN YOU ADD THE PATTERN.

SO WHAT YOU ARE SAYING IS THAT PEOPLE MUST FIRST POSSESS VIRTUE, AND THEN THEY SHOULD ADD PROPRIETY AS ADORNMENT.

YOU HAVE ENLIGHTENED ME! POETRY CAN ONLY BE DISCUSSED WITH EXTREMELY BRIGHT PEOPLE LIKE YOURSELF!

卜商字子夏，少孔子四十四歲。子夏問：『巧笑倩兮，美目盼兮，素以為絢兮』，何謂也？」子曰：「繪事後素。」曰：「禮後乎？」孔子曰：「商始可與言詩已矣。」子貢問：「師與商孰賢？」子曰：「師也過，商也不及。」「然則師愈與？」曰：「過猶不及。」子謂子夏曰：「汝為君子儒，無為小人儒。」孔子既沒，子夏居西河教授，為魏文侯師。其子死，哭之失明。

155

**SURNAME:** TANTAI
**GIVEN NAME:** MIEMING
**COMING-OF-AGE NAME:** ZIYU
**HOME STATE:** LU, CITY OF WU
**YEARS YOUNGER THAN CONFUCIUS:** THIRTY-NINE

TANTAI MIEMING WAS KNOWN TO HAVE A PHYSIQUE AND COUNTENANCE THAT WERE QUITE UGLY. DESPITE THIS, HOWEVER, HE WAS A MAN OF INTEGRITY. HE TRAVELED TO SOUTHERN CHINA WITH A FOLLOWING OF ABOUT THREE HUNDRED DISCIPLES. HE ESTABLISHED A CODE OF CONDUCT FOR THEM, WHICH HE HIMSELF NEVER VIOLATED. FOR THESE REASONS, HIS STERLING REPUTATION SPREAD TO NOBLEMEN IN THE FOUR CORNERS OF THE LAND.

ZIYOU WAS THE CHIEF MAGISTRATE OF THE CITY OF WU.

HAVE YOU HAD THE HELP OF ANY CAPABLE AND VIRTUOUS MEN THERE?

THERE IS ONE CALLED TANTAI MIEMING WHO IS STRICTLY LAW-ABIDING. HE NEVER TAKES SHORT-CUTS,

AND HE ONLY COMES TO MY RESIDENCE FOR OFFICIAL BUSINESS.

澹臺滅明，武城人，字子羽。少孔子三十九歲。

狀貌甚惡。欲事孔子，孔子以為材薄。既已受業，退而修行，行不由徑，非公事不見卿大夫。

南游至江，從弟子三百人，設取予去就，名施乎諸侯。孔子聞之，曰：「吾以言取人，失之宰

予；以貌取人，失之子羽。」

156

**SURNAME:** ZENG
**GIVEN NAME:** SHEN
**COMING-OF-AGE NAME:** ZIYU
**HOME STATE:** LU, SOUTHERN PART OF THE CITY OF WU
**YEARS YOUNGER THAN CONFUCIUS:** FORTY-SIX

CONFUCIUS SAW IN ZENGZI A GREAT PROPENSITY TOWARD FILIAL VIRTUE AND SO TRANSMITTED TO HIM ALL THAT HE KNEW ABOUT THE SUBJECT. ZENGZI THEN WROTE THE *BOOK OF FILIAL VIRTUE.* HE DIED LATE IN THE STATE OF LU.

ZENGZI, THERE IS ONE THREAD CONNECTING ALL MY THOUGHT.

YES, MASTER.

WHAT WAS HE REFERRING TO?

HE WAS REFERRING TO TWO WORDS: CONSCIENTIOUSNESS AND THOUGHTFULNESS!

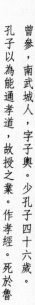

曾參，南武城人，字子輿。少孔子四十六歲。孔子以為能通孝道，故授之業。作孝經。死於魯。

157

**SURNAME:** YOU
**GIVEN NAME:** RUO
**COMING-OF-AGE NAME:** ZIYOU
**HOME STATE:** LU
**YEARS YOUNGER THAN CONFUCIUS:** FORTY-THREE

AFTER CONFUCIUS DIED, HIS DISCIPLES MISSED HIM VERY MUCH. BECAUSE YOU RUO RESEMBLED CONFUCIUS IN APPEARANCE, THEY CHOSE HIM TO BE THE NEW MASTER.

孔子既沒，弟子思慕，有若狀似孔子，弟子相與共立為師，師之如夫子時也。

有若少孔子四十三歲。有若曰：「禮之用，和為貴，先王之道斯為美。小大由之，有所不行；知和而和，不以禮節之，亦不可行也。」「信近於義，言可復也；恭近於禮，遠恥辱也；因不失其親，亦可宗也。」

THE PRACTICE OF PROPRIETY SHOULD EMPHASIZE HARMONY.

THE WAY OF THE KINGS OF ANTIQUITY, IN AFFAIRS SMALL AND LARGE, WAS TO ACT ACCORDING TO HARMONY.

BUT THIS IN ITSELF DID NOT ASSURE SUCCESS.

IF HARMONY IS NOT REGULATED BY PROPRIETY, IT CANNOT BE PUT INTO PRACTICE.

PROPRIETY

HARMONY

**SURNAME**: NANGONG
**GIVEN NAME**: KUO
**COMING OF AGE NAME**: ZIRONG
**HOME STATE**: LU
**AGE DIFFERENCE WITH CONFUCIUS**: UNKNOWN

CONFUCIUS SAID IN REGARD TO ZIRONG, "WHEN THE GOVERNMENT IS JUST, HE WILL CERTAINLY HOLD A POST. WHEN THE GOVERNMENT IS IN CHAOS, HE WILL MAINTAIN HIS INTEGRITY AND PROTECT HIMSELF FROM HARM." CONFUCIUS MARRIED HIS OWN NIECE TO HIM.

HOU YI WAS A GREAT ARCHER, AND AO COULD ROW A BOAT OVER LAND. BOTH OF THEM WERE MIGHTY AND COURAGEOUS, BUT NEITHER DIED A NATURAL DEATH.

XIA YU AND HOU JI, HOWEVER, WERE NOT LIKE THIS. THEY PERSONALLY TILLED THE FIELDS AND ENDED UP BEING LORDS OF THE WHOLE LAND. ISN'T THAT RIGHT?

CONFUCIUS DIDN'T ANSWER, AND ZIRONG DEPARTED.

THIS MAN IS TRULY A GENTLE-MAN! HOW HE ESTEEMS VIRTUE!

南宮括字子容。

問孔子曰：「羿善射，奡盪舟，俱不得其死然；禹稷躬稼而有天下？」孔子弗答。容出，孔子曰：「君子哉若人！」「國有道，不廢；國無道，免於刑戮。」三復「白珪之玷」，以其兄之子妻之。

159

公西赤字子華。少孔子四十二歲。

子華使於齊，冉有為其母請粟。孔子曰：「與之釜。」請益，曰：「與之庾。」冉子與之粟五

秉。孔子曰：「赤之適齊也，乘肥馬，衣輕裘。吾聞君子周急不繼富。」

●以上節自漢司馬遷史記仲尼弟子列傳

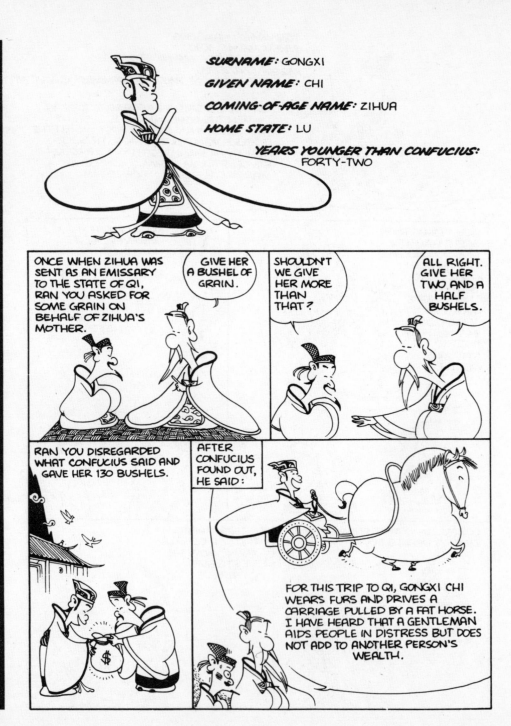

SURNAME: GONGXI

GIVEN NAME: CHI

COMING-OF-AGE NAME: ZIHUA

HOME STATE: LU

YEARS YOUNGER THAN CONFUCIUS: FORTY-TWO

ONCE WHEN ZIHUA WAS SENT AS AN EMISSARY TO THE STATE OF QI, RAN YOU ASKED FOR SOME GRAIN ON BEHALF OF ZIHUA'S MOTHER.

GIVE HER A BUSHEL OF GRAIN.

SHOULDN'T WE GIVE HER MORE THAN THAT?

ALL RIGHT. GIVE HER TWO AND A HALF BUSHELS.

RAN YOU DISREGARDED WHAT CONFUCIUS SAID AND GAVE HER 130 BUSHELS.

AFTER CONFUCIUS FOUND OUT, HE SAID:

FOR THIS TRIP TO QI, GONGXI CHI WEARS FURS AND DRIVES A CARRIAGE PULLED BY A FAT HORSE. I HAVE HEARD THAT A GENTLEMAN AIDS PEOPLE IN DISTRESS BUT DOES NOT ADD TO ANOTHER PERSON'S WEALTH.

160

# Guide to Pronunciation

There are different systems of romanization of Chinese words, but in all of these systems the sounds of the letters used do not necessarily correspond to those sounds which we are accustomed to using in English (for instance, would you have guessed that *zh* is pronounced like *j*?). Of course, these systems can be learned, but to save some time and effort for the reader who is not a student of Chinese, we have provided the following pronunciation guide. The Chinese words appear on the left as they do in the text and are followed by their pronunciations. Just sound out the pronunciations and you will be quite close to the proper Mandarin Chinese pronunciation.

## Notes:

*-dz* is a combination of *d* and *z* in one sound, without the *ee* sound at the end; so it resembles the sound of a bee in flight with a slight *d* sound at the beginning.

*-ts* is mostly the *ss* sound with a slight *t* (minus the *ee*) sound at the beginning.


Ai: I

Ao: ow(as in n*ow*)


Baili Xi: buy-lee shee

Bi: bee

Bian: byen

Bigan: bee-gone

Bingguan: beeng-gwon

Boyi: bwo(*o* as in m*o*re)-ee


Cai: tsigh(rhymes with high)

Cao: tsow(rhymes with now)

Chang Ju: chong jew(*ew* as in f*ew*)

Changping: chong-peeng

Chen: chun

Chen Huan: chun hwon

Chu: choo


Daye: dah(*a* as in f*a*ther)-yeh

Ding: deeng

Diqiu: dee-chyoh

Duanmu Si: dwon-moo sz


Gao Chai: gow(as in g*ow*n) chigh(rhymes with high)

Gao Yao: gow(as in g*ow*n) yow(rhymes with now)

Gao Zhaozi: gow(as in g*ow*n) jow(as in j*ow*l)-dz

Gonglian Chufu: gong(long o)-lyen choo-foo

Gongliang Ru: gong(long o)-lyong roo

Gongshan Buniu: gong(long o)-shon boo-nyoh

Gongshu: gong(long o)-shoo

Gongxi Chi: gong(long o)-shee chir

Gumie: goo-myeh

Gusu: goo-soo


Hou Ji: ho jee

Hou Yi: ho ee

Hu-lian: hoo-lyen

Huan: hwon

Huan Tui: hwon tway


Ji: jee

Ji Lu: jee loo

Jiagu: jyah(*a* as in f*a*ther)-goo

Jie Ni: jyeh nee

Jieyu: jyeh-ew(as in f*ew*)

Jin: jeen

Jing: jeeng

Jisun: jee-swoon(*oo* as in b*oo*k)

Jisun Fei: jee-swoon(*oo* as in b*oo*k) fay

Jisun Si: jee-swoon(*oo* as in b*oo*k) sz

Jisun Yiru: jee-swoon(*oo* as in b*oo*k) ee-roo

Ju: jew(*ew* as in f*ew*)


Kongfuzi: kong(long o)-foo-dz

Kong He: kong(long o) hu(*u* as in p*u*ll)

Kong Li: kong(long o) lee

Kong Qiu: kong(long o) chyoh

Kong Wenzi: kong(long o) wun-dz

Kuaiji: kwigh(rhymes with high)-jee

Kuang: kwong


Lai: lie

Laozi: lou(as in *lou*nge)-dz

Li Chu: lee choo

Ling: leeng

Linzi: leen-dz

Lu: loo

Luoyang: lwo(*o* as in m*o*re)-yong

Meng Gongchuo: mung gong(long o)-chwo(o as in more)

Meng Jingzi: mung jeeng-dz

Mengsun: mung-swoon(oo as in book)

Min: meen

Min Sun: meen swoon(oo as in book)

Min Ziqian: meen dz-chyen

Mu: moo


Nangong Jingshu: non-gong(long o) jeeng-shoo

Nangong Kuo: non-gong(long o) kwo(o as in more)

Nixi: nee-shee


Peng: pung

Pu: poo

Pu Shang: poo-shong


Qi: chee

Qin: cheen

Qu Boyu: chew(rhymes with few) bwo(o as in more)-ew(as in few)

Qufu: chew(rhymes with few)-foo

Ran: ron

Ran Boniu: ron bwo(*o* as in m*o*re)-nyoh

'Ran Qiu: ron chyoh

Ran Yong: ron yong(long o)

Ran You: ron yo

Ru Bei: roo bay

Shang: shong

Shangqiu: shong-chyoh

shao: shou(as in *shou*t)

Shaozheng Mao: shou(as in *shou*t)-jung mou(as in *mou*nt)

She: shu(*u* as in p*u*ll)

Shen Juxu: shun jew(*ew* as in f*ew*)-shew(*ew* as in f*ew*)

Shi Yu: sure ew(as in f*ew*)

Shimen: sure-mun

Shouyang: sho(long o)-yong

Shun: shwoon(*oo* as in b*oo*k)

Shuqi: shoo-chee

Shusun: shoo-swoon(*oo* as in b*oo*k)

Si: sz

Sicheng Zhenzi: sz-chung jun-dz

Sima Niu: sz-ma nyoh

Sima Qian: sz-ma chyen

Song: song(long o)


Tai: tie

Tang: tong

Tantai Mieming: ton(as in *ton*sil)-tie myeh-meeng

Taoqiu: tow(as in *tow*n)-chyoh

Tianchang: tyen-chong

Tsai Chih Chung: tsigh(rhymes with high) jir jong(long o)


Wanqiu: wan-chyoh

Wei: way

Wen: wun

Wu: oo


Xia: shyah(*a* as in *father*)

Xia Yu: shyah(*a* as in *father*) ew (as in *few*)

Xianyu: shyen-ew(as in *few*)

Xihe: shee hu(*u* as in p*u*ll)

Xinzheng: sheen-jung

Yan: yen

Yan Hui: yen hway

Yan Ke: yen ku(*u* as in p*u*ll)

Yan Shuzou: yen shoo-dzo(long o)

Yan Ying: yen eeng

Yan Yuan: yen ywen

Yang Huo: yong hwo(*o* as in m*o*re)

Yao: yow(rhymes with now)

Yi: ee

Ying: eeng

Yong: yong(long o)

You: yo

You Ruo: yo rwo(*o* as in m*o*re)

Yu: ew(as in f*ew*)

Yuan Rang: ywen rong

Yuan Xian: yewn shyen

Yue: yweh

Yue Qi: yweh chee


Zai: dzigh(rhymes with high)

Zai Wo: dzigh(rhymes with high) wo(*o* as in m*o*re)

Zai Yu: dzigh(rhymes with high) ew(as in f*ew*)

Zang Wuzhong: dzong oo-jong(long o)

Zeng: dzung

Zeng Shen: dzung shun

Zengzi: dzung-dz

Zhao: jow(as in *jow*l)

Zheng: jung

Zhong Gong: jong(long o) gong(long o)

Zhong You: jong(long o) yo

Zhongdu: jong(long o)-doo

Zhonggong: jong(long o)-gong(long o)

Zhongshan: jong(long o)-shon

Zhou: joe

Zhu: joo

Zhuangzi: jwong-dz

Zhuansun Shi: jwon-swoon(*oo* as in b*oo*k) sure

Zichan: dz-chon

Zigong: dz-gong(long o)

Zihua: dz-hwah(*a* as in f*a*ther)

Zilu: dz-loo

Ziqian: dz-chyen

Zirong: dz-rong(long o)

Ziwo: dz-wo(o as in more)

Zixia: dz-shyah(a as in father)

Ziyou: dz-yo

Ziyu: dz-ew(as in few)

Ziyuan: dz-ywen

Zizhang: dz-jong

Zou: dzo(long o)

Zuoqiu Ming: dzwo(o as in more)-chyoh meeng

# Glossary

**Benevolence:** As in English, the Chinese concept of benevolence (*ren*) is a general desire to promote the happiness of others, but Confucius specifically places it within the limits of propriety: "Benevolence is overcoming one's selfish desires and acting in accordance with propriety" (p. 96).

It is interesting to note that whereas in English we tend to think of specific virtues as applicable by all and to the same degree, Confucius felt that one's duty depends on one's social station. So a king's scope of benevolence would necessarily be much broader than the average person's. And unlike the Christian concept of love, not everyone was due the same consideration under all circumstances: Confucius said, "If you repay an enemy with kindness, how will you repay someone who is kind to you?" (p. 109).

**Ceremony:** See "Propriety" below.

**Conscientiousness:** In carrying out actions, one should be careful to "achieve one's intent" (the literal meaning of *zhong*). *Zhong* later came to be the common word for "loyalty."

**Filial virtue:** Often translated as filial piety, *xiao* refers to a child's (of any age) fulfilling the spirit of propriety in regard to his or her parents. It is the virtue of fulfilling one's filial duties.

**Gentleman:** The evolutions of the words "gentleman" and *"junzi"* are surprisingly similar. Both originally referred to nobility and later came to depict an exemplary man well regarded for his social station and proper conduct. It is this sense of the word that is used here. Confucius took the idea of a nobleman and extended it to mean that any man who acts in accordance with virtue and propriety should be considered a noble man, i.e., a gentleman. He contrasted the gentleman with the lesser man (*xiao ren*, literally a small person). The evolution of the Chinese word halted here and has since retained its meaning as the philosophical ideal of a man, unlike the English "gentleman," which has now been watered down to mean any polite man. So keep in mind that when Confucius speaks of a gentleman, he is referring to an exemplary man who lives in accord with the true spirit of virtue and propriety and follows the Way.

**Heaven:** Confucius often refers to Heaven, and in so doing he seems to be invoking fate. At the very least, Heaven for him appears to be a kind of intractable power that orders the universe. It is clear that he did believe in spiritual beings, but what marks Confucius' approach toward Heaven as significant is his dispensing with superstition and his insistence that all people can make a difference in bringing order to the world through their actions.

**Propriety:** Propriety is the central Confucian concept, the one that is most identifiably Confucian and most influential in Confucian thinking. To act in accord with propriety is to act in a manner suitable to one's social position. For us, propriety is typically a matter of performing (or not performing) certain actions under certain circumstances (like removing a hat indoors), but for Confucius, it is also a matter of carrying out one's duties to others based on specific relationships—i.e., parent-child, younger brother–older brother, husband-wife, minister-sovereign, friend-friend—the purpose being to establish and maintain harmony among all. In addition to the complex code of etiquette, it is also a general prescription of propriety that a child carry out filial duties to parents, that a minister perform his offices conscientiously, that a younger person treat an elder with due respect, etc.

The meaning of the Chinese word *li* is actually best expressed in English by using two words—propriety and ceremony. Ceremony, in English as well as in Chinese, is a ritualized form of social interaction, including interaction with deities.

**Righteousness:** When we think of righteousness in English, we think of actions that are valiantly just or moral. This is also the way the Chinese concept of the word *yi* later evolved, but in Confucius' time it referred to actions that were right in terms of the spirit of propriety. In fact, the two times the term occurs in this book (pp.104 and 120) it is rendered as "what is right." Instead of blindly following set rules of propriety, however, Confucian righteousness is the general idea of consciously fulfilling one's roles in society with substantial consideration given to reflective choice made according to each unique situation.

**Thoughtfulness:** In relations with everyone, one should strive to "compare hearts" (the literal meaning of *shu*). Confucius defines thoughtfulness with his version of the golden rule: "What you, yourself, do not like do not impose on others" (p.116).

**Way:** This is the same word rendered in *Zhuangzi Speaks* and *The Tao Speaks* as "Dao." Because there is no English equivalent that comes near the Daoist meaning of the word, it is left in its romanized form for those texts. Confucius, however, doesn't seem to imply the same metaphysical sense in his usage, so for his work, the English "Way" is preferable. Just as in English, the Chinese *"Dao"* means both a path and a method. What is interesting about Confucius' use of the word is that not only does he use it for particular instances of the right method of doing something, but he often speaks of "the Way" as though referring to one overarching system of principles. He never defines *"Dao,"* but it is apparent from his usage that he is referring to the sagely way of living virtuously as demonstrated by the sage kings of the past, and he sees it as his duty to transmit that Way.

**Worthy:** The term "worthy" is largely avoided in translating *xian* for this book. The reasoning is that although *xian* is very close in meaning to "worthy," the sense in which it is similar has largely gone out of use in English. Confucius uses the term as a noun, and in English we used to have the "nine worthies," but this usage seems to have disappeared. Therefore, the term is translated as it is defined in Chinese and used in adjectival form—"capable and virtuous."

## Reference Works

Chan, Wing-tsit. *A Source Book in Chinese Philosophy*. Princeton: Princeton University Press, 1969.

Fung, Yu-lan (Derk Bodde, tr.). *A History of Chinese Philosophy*. Princeton: Princeton University Press, 1952.

Graham, A. C. *Disputers of the Tao*. La Salle, IL: Open Court, 1989.

Hall, David L., and Roger T. Ames. *Thinking Through Confucius*. Albany, NY: State University of New York Press, 1987.

Schwartz, Benjamin I. *The World of Thought in Ancient China*. Cambridge, MA: Harvard University Press, 1985.

Confucius' Own Ideas:

Zheng Ming: rectification of names - each person must meet
definition of their title to do their job. If emporor
does not meet the 3 Aims, he is not emporor

Ren: human heartedness - individual related to pluralistic
society, all related to each other. Love others
& find harmoneous path

Yi: right, righteousness. There is an innate sense of 'right'
in humans even before we conceptualize "rightness."

Zhong: center heart, golden-mean. Do what you would have
done to you.

Shu: like heartedness. Share other's suffering - sympathy. Do not
do what you would not have done to you.

Ming: fate, destiny. Human life is limited & precence is finite -
do the best you can to make things better w/in
your limits & circumstances

Dao: path thru reality. "If I find the truth in the morning,
I am ready to die in the evening." Truth.
Personal ethics + social philosophy combined.

Xiao: a) fillial piety
b) work hard to become civil servant & order society
c) cultivate character & seek learning

# About the Authors

**Tsai Chih Chung** is a Taiwanese cartoonist and popularizer of Chinese philosophy whose books have sold over eighteen million copies and have been translated into a dozen languages. In addition to *Confucius Speaks*, *The Tao Speaks*, *Zen Speaks*, *Sunzi Speaks* (all from Anchor Books), and *Zhuangzi Speaks* (Princeton University Press) have been translated into English. Tsai Chih Chung divides his time between Taiwan and Vancouver.

**Brian Bruya** is a professional translator with a B.A. in philosophy and Chinese from the University of Washington. He lives in Seattle, Washington.

Keep in mind these other books by Tsai Chih Chung and translated by Brian Bruya, also available from Anchor Books:

*Zen Speaks: Shouts of Nothingness* 0-385-47257-9
*Sunzki Speaks: The Art of War* 0-385-47258-7
*The Tao Speaks: Lao-Tzu's Whispers of Wisdom* 0-385-47259-5